VOLUNTEERS FOR THE GALLOWS

ANATOMY OF A SHOW-TRIAL

Volunteers for the Gallows

ANATOMY OF A SHOW-TRIAL

BY
Béla Szász

Translated by
KATHLEEN SZÁSZ

W · W · NORTON & COMPANY · INC ·
NEW YORK

None of the persons mentioned in this book are invented. All are, or were, alive.

Contents

1 The T-Shaped Table   *page* 1

2 To Sleep Or Not To Sleep   18

3 The People's Educator   50

4 'Imperialist Agent. Establish This!'   67

5 The Governor Appears On The Scene   93

6 Prefabricated Elements   113

7 Political Iconography   133

8 The People Judge   165

9 Which Is Mine?   185

10 The Funeral Of An Era   216

Postscript   240

VOLUNTEERS FOR THE GALLOWS

ANATOMY OF A SHOW-TRIAL

I

The T-Shaped Table

THE building housing the Budapest Ministry of Agriculture, erected some two hundred years ago in the days of the Empress Maria Theresa, was originally intended for a barracks. However, few people in Hungary recall this symbolic historical prelude, for, as long ago as our grandfathers' days those concerned with agriculture in Hungary were looking for guidance towards this same shabby and patched-up neo-classical building and it was from here they awaited–for many generations in vain–some solution of the country's agrarian problems.

A generous, even extravagant broad flight of stairs and a wide corridor lead to the rooms of the Minister, the Undersecretaries and department heads which are situated in the front of the building, while the side-wings and the back are criss-crossed with windowless, narrow passages sparingly illuminated by tiny electric bulbs. Even in 1949, the rooms still smelt of dusty bundles of files pushed back and forth for decades, and the ghosts of bureaucrats, dead for a hundred years, haunted the archives.

When at the end of 1948 I was appointed head of the press and information department, my room opened neither on to the elegant principal gallery nor the depressing criss-cross corridors. Journalists visiting me entered from the main staircase into a spacious hall.

On the 24th of May, 1949, about half-past nine in the morning, a few Hungarian and a number of foreign journalists assembled in this hall. We were about to visit a once world-famous Hungarian stud-farm. I had invited B. J. B. Groeneveld, the Dutch agricultural attaché, to join the excursion, for, being the only agricultural attaché in the entire Western diplomatic corps and thus having little

I

opportunity to visit agricultural research centres or discuss matters in his particular field, he must have felt lonely and isolated in Budapest. He used to come and see me almost every week, asking questions with tact and circumspection, for even then he must have been far more keenly aware than I was of the precariousness of my situation.

Groeneveld and I were sitting in my room, in deep leather armchairs placed under the window, and he was asking me about the experiments of the Hungarian agronomist, Kurt Sedelmeyer, when the official whose job it was to organize our expedition announced that everything was ready for our departure. Accredited foreign correspondents usually came in their own cars but visiting journalists and Hungarian newspapermen travelled in the automobiles provided by the Ministry. I had accepted Groeneveld's invitation to share his car, although this was already frowned on as a form of fraternization with the West. I had taken my place at his side and the engine was running, when one of the clerks of the press department tapped the window and informed me that Géza Losonczy, the Undersecretary of State, had sent over two Argentinian journalists to see me. No-one apart from myself spoke Spanish in the department and the two journalists were leaving next day.

I had spent seven years in Argentina and was interested in what my Argentinian colleagues could tell me about Buenos Aires. So I went without hesitation. I apologized to Groeneveld for deserting him and promised to arrange for him to see Kurt Sedelmeyer. Then I got out of the car and returned to the building. The promise I gave to Groeneveld remains to this day unfulfilled.

I found the Argentinians standing in the hall, somewhat at a loss. I joined them and we waited for the lift. In Hungary, in office buildings as well as in blocks of flats, the lift takes passengers up only; they have to descend on foot. This is how it came about that while the obsolete contraption was taking us up to the first floor, three ÁVH* investigators who had been looking for me during my brief absence from my office, were going down the stairs. A few minutes earlier, as Groeneveld and I had walked down to the car, these same three secret police had been crammed in the tiny lift, going up. This fact I reconstructed, in part, five or six hours later from hints dropped by the investigators, in part five or six years later from the recollections of my former secretary.

One of the ÁVH men introduced himself to my secretary as a journalist; she told him that my party and I would be back about

* ÁVH — Államvedelmi Hatóság: State Security Authority, the Hungarian political police.

2

three o'clock in the afternoon. She did not mention the matter to me
when I returned a few minutes later to my office, as she thought it
completely unimportant. She did not, of course, know that in the
morning I had had a call asking me to be at Party Headquarters at
about two thirty, as there were a few things to discuss before the
3 o'clock meeting. I had a long session with the Argentinians, then, a
few minutes before half-past two, I set out towards the nearby Party
Headquarters. At the same time, one of the three ÁVH men showed
up again at my office, asking for me.

In 1945, the Hungarian Communist Party had appropriated for its
offices the building of No. 17, Akadémia Street. Soon, the neighbouring block of flats was requisitioned. And then it swallowed up
several more blocks, but its appetite was still unsatisfied; it removed
more and more families from their flats and constantly shifted and
re-built its offices. Instead of permanent revolution, it lived in a
fever of permanent removal. In May, 1949, the Rural Propaganda
department occupied a newly-furnished, attractive suite of rooms at
Party Headquarters.

The assistant head of the department was called János Kukucska.
He had never changed his quaint Slovak peasant name–it means
Peeping John–believing, probably, that being the possessor of a
name that everyone remembered at first hearing must benefit his
career. This farmhand turned Party official emphasized his peasant
origin by wearing high boots and a lambskin cap, although neither
his urban way of living nor the climate of the capital warranted this
outfit. In addition to his peasant background and quick mind, this
smiling young man was assured of a vertiginous career by his
capacity to agree readily and enthusiastically with the views of his
superiors, even when they conflicted with his own experience and
the obvious facts.

We sat facing each other across his desk. But no sooner had we
begun talking than we were interrupted by the ringing of the telephone. He lifted the receiver and handed it to me:

'Comrade Keresztes's secretary is asking for you.'

Mihály Keresztes, Communist Undersecretary of Agriculture,
really ran the Hungarian agricultural administration; István Csala,
the Smallholder Party Minister of Agriculture, was a mere figure-
head and was regarded as such by all officials in the Ministry. Csala
attended receptions, driven in a huge automobile, and articles signed
with his name appeared in the newspapers–articles that he had
perhaps not even read–but in the Ministry his voice carried no more
weight than that of the doorman. Although the multi-party system

3

had not yet been liquidated, the Ministry was already controlled by the Communist Party through Mihály Keresztes.

As Keresztes was leaving that day for the Soviet Union with a peasant delegation, it seemed reasonable that he should have remembered something that had to be taken care of at the last moment. However, his secretary did not connect me with him, but merely informed me that the Peasant Party member of parliament, Szücs, the other leader of the delegation, was in conference in Keresztes's room and wished to see me before his departure. 'All right,' I replied, 'I shall be back at the Ministry immediately the meeting at Party Headquarters is over.'

Two minutes later the telephone rang again.

'It's for you again.' Kukucska was annoyed. 'Tell them,' he added, 'that if it's so urgent, Szücs can come here and call you out of the meeting. We are going to begin in a minute.'

I repeated Kukucska's words to Keresztes's secretary and replaced the receiver. A minute later the telephone rang yet again. This time I answered it myself.

A male voice I had never heard before said, 'This is Szücs,' adding that he absolutely must see me at once to hand over some documents, but as he was waiting for important telephone calls in the Undersecretary's room, he could not leave. He would be obliged if I would come over for a few minutes. If I had no car at my disposal he would send his to fetch me. 'Don't be ridiculous,' I replied, 'I can walk a hundred and fifty yards. I'll come right away.'

'You can start the conference without me,' I told Kukucska, 'I'll be back in about fifteen minutes.'

This was the second promise I made that day and never kept. I was in such a hurry that I left not only my brief-case but also my raincoat in the Party official's room, despite the fact that the mild western wind had brought on a steady drizzle. The first week of May had held out a prospect of early summer but now, at the end of the month, I could have done with an overcoat.

I turned up the collar of my jacket and crossed the road with quick steps. I looked neither to the right nor to the left, even less behind me, and thus did not observe the thin, bespectacled fellow shadowing me. As soon as I reached the gallery leading to Keresztes's room, two men barred my way. One was short, greying, with regular features and a military bearing, the other tall, flabby and overfed with a strikingly brutal face.

4

They asked my name. I told them—Béla Szász. Then the grey-haired man presented his credentials.

'State Security,' he whispered stressing each syllable. 'Come with us, please.'

'What for?' I asked, surprised. 'Why don't you telephone if you want something from me?'

'It is a very urgent matter,' the younger of the two replied, putting his hand in his pocket and keeping it there.

It was obvious that protest would be useless and though I racked my brains in vain for an explanation, I went along with the two detectives, far from guessing that I was no longer even relatively free, for no Communist functionary had been arrested in Hungary since 1945. When old crimes were discovered or some act of corruption came to light, the case was first investigated by the Party's Control Committee, the guilty member was expelled, and only then did police procedure follow.

We started down the stairs. This time the ÁVH men had not missed me. The grey-haired man headed the procession, I followed and behind me, as rear-guard, the brutish-looking young man. Some people we passed smiled at me in greeting; it did not occur to any of them that here was a man who had reached the cross-roads of his life and was on his way towards exploring a hazy landscape that, though he didn't know it, had long been waiting his coming.

We left the building by the main entrance, then turned into a side street where a medium-sized car was waiting. Beside it stood the thin, bespectacled man. He opened the rear door without a word. My two companions made me sit between them; we were rather cramped. The bespectacled one took his place next to the driver.

'Where are we going?' I asked.

'To Headquarters,' the grey-haired detective replied and began a conversation with complete ease, as if we were sitting in a drawing-room. He told me we had once met at a reception where I was talking to someone about mediaeval Spanish plays. Did I remember? I did not. My cool reply did not deter him, he went on talking, smiling, as if we were the best of friends.

The car drew up at the entrance to 60, Andrássy Street. Before 1945, this building had been the headquarters of the Arrow-Cross Party, the fortress of Hungarian fascism. In 1945 it had been occupied by the political police and gradually, just like Party Head-quarters, it had swallowed up the neighbouring buildings, then the entire block and finally all the tenants were evicted from the side-streets. The entrances and street-corners were guarded by uniformed security men with tommy-guns, and at the Andrássy Street entrance to ÁVH Headquarters the citizens of the people's democracy were kept at a distance by heavy iron chains slung between squat, concrete posts. From the tops of the small posts and from the window-sills of the Andrássy Street façade, red geraniums nodded their flaming heads towards the tommy-guns.

The detectives showed their credentials, then took me up on foot to the first floor. From the main corridor we turned into a panelled lobby hung with mirrors and decorated with the sort of carvings that the South-East European *nouveau riche* filled his hall with at the turn of the century.

'We are going to see Comrade Péter,' the bespectacled man said almost kindly, and he opened a door.

Lieutenant-General Gábor Péter was Head of the political police. He and I had met several times, mainly at official receptions. Like most militants of the former underground Communist movement, we used the familiar second person singular when talking to each other. Péter's long, narrow waiting-room was furnished with a desk and two drawing-room suites. The grey-haired investigator pointed to a deep, purple armchair:

'Please sit down . . .'

I sat down.

'I should like to call the Ministry,' I said, 'for I was told that Deputy Szücs is waiting for me in the Undersecretary's room.'

I put no stress on the words 'I was told', for I was not yet convinced that it was the ÁVH-men who had telephoned me in Szücs's name. The three men exchanged glances. 'I'll ring them right away,' the flabby young man offered, 'and tell them you'll be there in about half an hour.'

He opened the double padded door of his chief's room and disappeared behind it. I lit a cigarette but did not offer one to my companions. Besides us there was only an obviously bored, blond youth in the waiting-room. His epaulettes showed him to be a lieutenant. He rested his elbows on his desk and fiddled with the telephone. Five or six minutes went by, then the detective returned.

'Let's go,' he told his colleagues. Then he turned to me, 'I called the Ministry,' he said reassuringly.

We left the building. A powerful American Buick was waiting at the door. Only after we had taken our places in the car did I notice that all the windows, including the back-window and that separating the driver from the passengers, were shrouded from the outside world by black curtains. Again they made me sit between the grey-

6

haired man and the brutal-faced detective and when, with a sudden jerk, the car sprang into motion, the grey-haired one said:

'We shall now blindfold you.'

'Do we have to play cops and robbers?' I asked, vexed.

'You ought to be glad,' the detective replied, reaching for a folded napkin obviously prepared in advance, 'for if we blindfold you, there's at least a chance that you may come back . . .'

This was the first, though still mild and veiled, threat; until now they had treated me with awkward politeness, a clumsy pretence of friendliness, as if it were important to them that I should have no reason to complain of their treatment of me. But even now, the detective's words appeared to me a childishly romantic taunt rather than a prophecy heralding real dangers. I made no reply but lit another cigarette. I deduced from various sounds that the car crossed a bridge over the Danube, then took the steep road up one of the Buda mountains, at such speed that the tyres squealed at every turn and I bumped now against one, now against the other of my neighbours.

We raced on for about half an hour but now none of us spoke. Finally we must have turned into a side-road for the motor slowed down and soon afterwards we stopped. The front door of the car opened and slammed. I heard the grating of a metal gate, then we were rolling over gravel, there was a soft thud, and then the hum of the motor grew louder indicating that we had driven into a garage. Although the driver switched off the engine, neither of my companions made any move to get out. There was a heavy, dull silence. Only my sense of smell found something to report: a pervading odour of petrol and oil. I could see nothing through the bandage but presumably a light-signal must have flashed for not only my two neighbours but also the detective in front sprang simultaneously into action.

They helped me out of the car, one took my right arm, one my left, and we started down a flight of stairs. But as there was not room for the three of us on the narrow stairs, and as the rhythm of our steps did not coincide, we groped, now pushing and pulling, now crowding in on one another in an oblique formation, deeper and deeper down. When we reached the bottom, the men let go of my arm. An iron door banged shut behind me and the bandage was ripped roughly from my eyes.

Five or six savage-looking men surrounded me.

'Traitor!' a short, round-faced man hissed in my face.

'You rat!' another whispered almost inaudibly, baring his teeth.

7

What surprised me was that the faces of these men appeared not so much angry as gloomy and worried. I felt as if I were surrounded by a bunch of outwardly adult but mentally immature creatures, about to commit a murder from fear.

'Have you searched him?' one of them asked. 'Is he armed?' Then he turned to me with a command:

'Strip to your shirt and pants.'

They explored even the hem of my underclothes, took away all my possessions, my wallet, fountain-pen, cigarettes, lighter, wrist-watch, belt, shoe-laces; I was allowed to keep only my handkerchief. I was standing with my back to the iron door through which we had entered. To the left were three smaller iron doors and, opposite, the passage grew wider. As soon as I was dressed again they unlocked the first small iron door and pushed me in.

I found myself in a cell in which I could not stand upright because of the low, vaulted roof. The cell was approximately six feet long and two and a half feet wide; attached to the right wall by iron brackets was a one and a half inch thick board on which lay a folded horse-blanket. A man of medium height could only have sat hunched up on the bunk, which was fitted waist-high to the wall; even if he pressed his chin to his chest his head would hit the cellar roof.

The walls and the iron door were constantly covered with fat drops of water which every so often swelled into rivulets and set out on their suicidal course along the path laid down by their predecessors. The air was palpably humid and the blanket had absorbed so much of the damp that it felt like a sponge fished out of a bathtub. A naked bulb glowed in a square recess over the iron door but it only irritated the eye without dispelling the darkness of the cell.

While I was taking stock of my surroundings my gaolers peeped in several times through the Judas-hole, but after a brief five or six minutes the key turned in the lock and I found myself once more in the passage. I was searched again. One of the detectives asked his companions whether they were certain I had no weapon hidden on me, then two of them led the way, two placed themselves on my right and left, and one walked behind me jabbing his gun into my backbone and ordering me to put my hands on the nape of my neck. In this way our little group advanced towards the end of the passage. Then we mounted a flight of concrete steps to the ground floor and thence, up wooden stairs, to the first floor.

Here the staircase widened. Again, the windows were hung with black curtains shutting out daylight and the outside world. Above a double door, coloured bulbs glowed. They must have signalled

8

'pass', for the young detective entered without knocking. A moment later he returned and nodded to the others. The door opened wide to admit me.

I found myself in an enormous room. Its numerous windows were draped in black. Opposite the double door they had pushed together two long narrow refectory tables in the shape of a capital T. The semi-circular, black-curtained window recess behind the upper, horizontal line of the T created a theatrical effect and optically lengthened the stem of the T extending towards the entrance.

My attendants made me stand at the bottom of the T, then withdrew. Far away, behind the top stroke of the T sat five men, some in uniform, some in civilian clothes. In the centre was Gábor Péter, head of the secret political police. Of the other four I knew only one, Colonel Ernö Szücs, Péter's deputy. Péter looked at me grimly and asked:

'Which espionage organization have you been working for?'

'Now really . . .' I replied breaking into laughter, partly because these dignitaries enthroned behind the T-shaped table looked ludicrous enough, partly because it didn't even occur to me to take Péter's question seriously and therefore, I drew the only possible conclusion, namely that I was the victim of some childish prank, that they were playing a game, making a fool of me. I was not concerned that Péter had dropped the familiar second person singular and addressed me as though I were a stranger: perhaps that was part of the joke too. When I replied, I addressed him by his first name.

'Don't make me laugh, Gábor . . .'

'We'll see who has the last laugh,' Gábor Péter shouted jumping up from his chair, 'when we come to your contemptible doings in South America.' Then he sat down again, glaring at me.

'Who is Wagner?' he asked, smiling ironically with the air of one dealing a death blow to his enemy.

'Wagner?' I mused, recalling first the music teacher of my school days, then an old acquaintance, a historian, deported by the Nazis. Neither could be the Wagner in whom Péter seemed interested. Then suddenly it came to me:

'Do you mean the Hungarian consul in Bratislava?' I asked. 'I know him only superficially . . .'

Péter waved his hand and, as if this had been a cue, the others sitting at the head of the table broke into a chorus of synthetic police-laughter.

'No, that isn't the Wagner I am thinking of,' Péter said with a drawl. 'I am thinking of the Wagner from whom you brought Szönyi an illegal message with a password!'

9

'Tibor Szönyi!' I exclaimed, surprised because, as far as I knew, Szönyi was still head of the Communist Party's cadres department, a post carrying at least ministerial rank in the state administration, as it was the cadres department that suggested, or even decided on its own authority, to what posts Communist Party-members should be appointed in the state administration, the Party, the army, or the so-called mass-organizations. When I was transferred from the Foreign Ministry to the Ministry of Agriculture, it had been Tibor Szönyi and his assistant, András Szalai, who informed me of the decision and discussed it with me. Szönyi had explained to me, in a dull party-jargon hardly in keeping with his erudition and intellect, why, though I knew next to nothing about agrarian problems, it was important that I should assume the direction of the press department of the Ministry of Agriculture instead of remaining at the Foreign Ministry. Had someone really brought this cold, rigid party functionary an 'illegal' message? Even supposing this someone was I, why should we have used a password as we did in the underground Communist movement, when contact had to be established between two party members or fellow-travellers who did not know each other? I repeated my train of thought aloud, but Péter interrupted impatiently:

'You'd better tell us the password.'

'I know of no password.'

'Then let me tell you what it was. It was 'Wagner notifies Péter. And what was the message?'

'I don't know anything about a password or a message.'

'Fetch Szönyi,' Gábor Péter ordered.

Any development of this farce would have surprised me less than Szönyi's appearance. Yet he appeared. Seconds later, there stood on my right, also at the foot of the T, the head of the Communist Party's cadres department, in a somewhat crumpled grey suit and a blue jersey sports shirt without a tie.

'Did this man bring you a message?'

'Yes, he did' Szönyi nodded, taking care not to look at me.

'One with a password?'

'Yes. One with a password.'

'What was the password? Tell him to his face!'

Szönyi, though he turned his face towards me, avoided my eyes.

'Wagner notifies Péter,' he said.

'And when did I give you that message?'

Szönyi looked up in perplexity, his gaze crept up from my shoes to my face, then slid away above my head. He stared into the air as if he were thinking, then said slowly, in a low voice:

'Last year, on the 4th of May.'

'And where did I give it to you?'

'In my office,' Szönyi replied, this time without hesitation.

'Well,' I said, relieved, 'this makes matters infinitely more simple. I went to see Szönyi quite a few times, so I know that his office keeps a record of every incoming telephone call, whether Szönyi takes it or not, and of every visitor, whether he is received by Szönyi or passed on to one of his subordinates. This record will show whether or not I saw Szönyi on the 4th of May last year. And there is something else too! As I had no permanent pass, I would have had to ask for an entrance slip at the gate. If I entered Party Headquarters at that period there must be a record of it. Unless I had business there, I didn't go to Party Headquarters for months at a time, so it should take you only a few minutes to find out that Szönyi is not telling the truth.'

'Do you maintain your statement?' Péter turned to Szönyi.

'I do.'

'And you too?' he asked me.

'Naturally.'

'In that case,' Gábor Péter shrugged impatiently, 'give them both a soling.'

Soling, an expression borrowed from the shoemaking industry, was already used in the vocabulary of the pre-war Hungarian police to describe an ancient but piously preserved mode of interrogation. The bare soles of the suspected person were beaten, first with a cane, later with a rubber truncheon, until he declared himself ready to confess. Szönyi presumably knew from experience what *soling* meant, for at Gábor Péter's words his features twisted into a plaintive begging expression, he raised his shoulders and held out his hands, palms upward, towards Péter in a gesture of helplessness, but a guard grasped his arm and led him out. This was my last meeting with the former head of the cadres department. Later, in one of the cells of the Markó Street prison, I discovered traces of his presence. He had scratched his name into the ancient layer of whitewash, connecting it skilfully, in a wreath of vines, with the words, 'Little Flower'; next to it he had kept a diary which showed that his arrest had taken place one week before mine. By the time I came across Szönyi's handwriting, my own bouquet of recollections and the words 'Little Flower' had reconciled me to him; but for the present I was still resentful, I was still angry with him, rather than the secret police, because I felt he was deliberately fooling Gábor Péter and his men and was accusing me falsely, perhaps to protect someone else.

I was still convinced of this when I entered the small room where a powerfully built man was waiting for me. Later I had occasion to see him repeatedly and from information gathered and remarks dropped, I discovered that his name was Detective Inspector Gyula Prinz, that once upon a time he had been a detective in Horthy's criminal police, but having supported the rather weak Hungarian resistance movement he was, after 1945, rewarded by being promoted detective-inspector in the ÁVH. Prinz, with the rubber truncheon swinging from his wrist, pointed almost apologetically, almost mildly, to the floor:

'Take off your shoes, please, and lie down on your stomach.'

We were alone in the room. Prinz muttered something and shrugged his shoulders with embarrassment. Perhaps it was his irresoluteness that disarmed me. After all, I thought, he's only obeying an order and I complied readily. Prinz hit the soles of my feet ten blows each with his truncheon. I took hold of myself so as not to groan but I think that if I bore this first *soling* more easily than the subsequent ones it was not merely because the truncheon came down on healthy, still unbroken skin, still uninjured tissues, but also because Prinz swung the truncheon from at most shoulder height, not in a three-quarter arc, like the experts I encountered later.

I was led back into the big room and again made to stand at the foot of the T.

'Well, do you admit it now?' Péter asked sneeringly.

'Szönyi is lying,' I replied, 'and you can prove it in half an hour if you examine the entrance slips at Party Headquarters and the diary of Szönyi's secretary . . .'

'I didn't ask you for advice. You had better realize that you can count on nobody's support, nobody's protection here. You understand? The Party has delivered you into our hands. Will you admit that you brought Szönyi an illegal message?'

'How can I admit it . . .'

'Give him some more of the same,' Péter shouted, pointing at the door.

This time I was taken to another room where I found myself surrounded by five or six men. I believe I never told anyone during my long imprisonment something that, at the time, seemed absolutely natural to me, namely, that when one of the detectives hit me in the face, I returned the blow with equal force. A couple of years later my action appeared improbable to me: more than that, as if invented by myself.

I was obeying some ancient impulse, maybe the bidding of my

upbringing, or perhaps I was living up to the code of honour prevalent in the provincial environment of my youth, though intellectually I regarded these interpretations of honour as comically obsolete and unrealistic. According to the standards of that code my first experience of the bastinado almost amounted to a voluntarily undergone test, but the first blow in the face was so obvious a humiliation that retaliation was instinctive, regardless of the consequences.

It did not take the five or six men long to overpower me with their fists, kicks and blows with truncheon and gun-butt. Then they stamped on me, sat astride my back, bent back my legs and held them while one of their colleagues beat my soles, swinging his truncheon through three-quarters of a circle. When I was led back to the big room I was unable to open my right eye and my face as well as my clothes bore witness to what had happened in the next room.

'What did you do to him?' Péter asked his men.

'He fell,' a rough voice behind me replied, drawing out and deepening the vowels so as to lend the answer, with its surburban overtones, a shade of vacuity.

The upper group at the T-shaped table rewarded this wit with hooting laughter, then Péter looked at me mockingly:

'Will you admit it now?'

'Not even if you put me through this treatment a hundred times. Szönyi is lying and you can easily prove it.'

'Take him away,' the head of the secret police commanded and my guards led me back, pushing and pulling me down the darkened staircase to the cellar, where they flung me into the cell.

While I was pacing to and fro in the little cell, or trying to squat on the bunk with my head between my shoulders, then lie on it with knees bent, two ÁVH squad-cars stopped in front of No. 11, Üllöi Street, the large block of flats where I lived. At a barked command, troops armed with rifles and tommy-guns jumped out. One group, so the inhabitants of the flats told me later, spread out in open formation, then cautiously, hugging the wall, worked their way up to my flat on the fifth floor. Armed troops occupied the landings, the back-stairs and, with an encircling manoeuvre, blocked the exits. Plain-clothes security men, accompanied by uniformed police with tommy-guns, opened my flat, and the search began.

What was the purpose of all this? When the squad-cars arrived I had been in the hands of the ÁVH for two solid hours. I think the principal aim was not to intimidate the civilian population, but to create tension in the ÁVH organisation and fill both officers and men with the sense of an immediate threat to their safety, if not their lives.

No ÁVH man could ever have supposed that his superiors would engage in such a large-scale operation as this raid on my flat in Üllöi Street, were it not to trap some utterly determined and unscrupulous conspirator.

After their military exercise they locked my rooms, then, for almost three months, two or three plain-clothes men visited the flat every day. The neighbours closely observed the ideological and practical results of these visits in the ÁVH's interpretation of the notion of private property; they always arrived with conspicuously flat briefcases and departed with equally conspicuously bulging ones. Key-hole inspection, systematically maintained by the neighbours in the absence of the ÁHV, noted the gradual disappearance of important pieces of criminal evidence, such as my table-lighter, candlesticks, embroidered cloths and such-like items.

About a hundred days later, the ÁVH must have grown tired of this piece-meal looting. Lorries arrived and took away those articles that wouldn't fit into briefcases: my furniture, pictures, carpets, books. They dismantled even the shutters in my little son's room and left nothing in mine except a small heap of rubbish, among it, a few photographs of my child.

All this I learned, of course, only half a decade later. At the time I was busy turning over in my mind every possible explanation of Szönyi's reasons for throwing such grave suspicion on me. It did not even occur to me that it might not have been Szönyi's accusations that compelled the ÁVH to act but, on the contrary, that ÁVH treatment might have compelled Szönyi to bear false witness.

Marking time in the cellar I still hoped that Gábor Péter would examine the diary of the cadres department's secretariat and the entrance slips issued by Party Headquarters, and if this part of Szönyi's statement proved untrue–for I had not visited the cadres department or even Party Headquarters on the 4th of May–Péter would give little credence to the second part of the statement, namely, that on that fictitious visit I had brought Szönyi an illegal message. However, the demeanour of the detectives when, long hours later, they at last opened the door of the oppressively airless cell, gave no hint of any such official doubts.

Again my four attendants led me towards the staircase. We passed the double door on the first floor, left the second floor behind, then climbed on up the narrowing staircase between black-curtained windows. To the right, in a recess, I noticed an iron door which, I suspected with a shudder of unreasoning fear, opened straight into the void. But we passed it, and half a storey higher, they pushed me into a six-sided room. Each wall of the room, except the one into which the door had been built, consisted of a huge, flat, oblong window, blind and dead-black like its fellows on the staircase. Yet the circle of windows indicated that we were in a tower-room from where a heart-warming view must open on the mountains of Buda and perhaps even the town below.

The detectives silently surrounded me. Then, one struck me across the back with his rubber truncheon. As if this were a sign, all fell upon me, threw me on the floor, stamped on me, kicked me all over my body. They did not aim at the sensitive, delicate spots with the cold, calculated expertise of professional batterers and torturers, with the sadism of those enjoying their craft, like many of my future interrogators, but acted rather like a party of drunks, intoxicated with rage. They hurled abuse at me and belaboured me ceaselessly with their truncheons. Not for a moment did their fury appear simulated. They considered it natural that I should try to defend myself and catch hold of one or other of the raised truncheons. So it was that at times we were all rolling around on the floor, arms, legs intertwined, then they would pull me to my feet and go on with their job until, at last, the grey-haired man threw himself into the only armchair in the tower-room and asked me, panting and wheezing:

'What was the message Wagner sent Péter?'

'Szönyi is lying. There was no message.'

Swinging the truncheon between his knees like the pendulum of a clock and pretending not to have heard my reply, the detective repeated his question with added emphasis:

'What was the message Wagner sent Péter?'

Then the voice of the young, fat one, cut in like a whip:

'When did you join the American secret service?'

The next question came in a screaming chorus:

'Who hired you?'

My denials brought them on me in full force; questioning alternated with attack, till finally they hurled me to the floor and concentrated their attention on my soles. Somehow I succeeded in shaking them off, upon which they rolled me into the carpet, with the help of a fifth man who had, until then, stood by the wall as a mere spectator. One knelt on the back of my neck, one sat astride my neck, and two raised the soles of my feet under the swinging truncheon. After twice twenty-five blows they unrolled the carpet and kicking, pushing, hitting the nape of my neck, compelled me to run in circles round the room. While I ran they kept firing the same questions at me, endlessly. In the meantime the fifth man had slunk from the room, but by the time the others had again rolled me into the carpet he returned with a large spoon full of salt. They prised apart my clenched teeth with a pocket knife and pushed the salt into my mouth, then concentrated on my feet again. Only now they no longer hit out with the energy-squandering passion of drunks, but used their muscles and truncheons with systematic economy. They beat my soles, my kidneys and the more sensitive parts of my body with expert skill.

The fifth man disappeared once more but I was to meet him again several times at this secret ÁVH villa. His function, it seemed, was that of caretaker and general help. He opened doors, catered for his superiors and stood guard when a prisoner was taken to the lavatory. This middle-aged, pot-bellied man reappeared later in our prison-life. His name was István Lehota. But just now his withdrawal did not mark the end of my first day, we had merely reached half-time in our evening gymnastics.

The ÁVH did not add to the three original questions – what was Wagner's message, when did I join the American secret service, and who recruited me – but they embellished them with far from complimentary adjectives, describing Wagner, myself, and particularly my female ancestry, with conspicuously poor imagination. Still, when one or another enriched the vocabulary with a new obscenity, the others howled it after him with enthusiasm. Nor did the methods of criminal investigation vary. They rolled me twice more into the carpet, to tickle my soles, as they said, in order to improve my memory, but finally, assuring me that I could look forward to much more convincing methods of memory-improvement, they led me down from the tower-room. Dawn was breaking. Through the open door of the lavatory the reflected light of a grey morning fell on the cellar steps.

A short man with a long nose and a trimmed moustache, wearing a sort of ski-cap and a fur-lined coat, stood idly before the cellar door. It was he who locked the cell door after me and from then on his sad, dark eyes appeared every four or five minutes at the Judas-hole. He watched me inspecting my swollen, black-and-blue soles and trying to find some way of settling down on the bunk so that the hard, narrow board should not intensify the pain. Half an hour later he opened the door.

'Do you want some water?'

I did. I raised myself with difficulty to a sitting position. My tongue and palate were still burning from the salt forced between my teeth. I swallowed two mouthfuls. The water tasted salty. I spat it out.

'What's the matter?' the man asked.

'It's salt.'

'You don't imagine I'd give you salt water to drink, do you?' he asked, offended.

He must have felt that I was repaying his almost illegal lenience with ingratitude. Mangled as I was and locked in a damp underground cell, I was still keenly aware of how comic was the parallel between his resentment and mine; I must have smiled, for the long-nosed one asked me in a harsh but low voice:

'Is there anything else you want?'

I asked him if he could leave the lid of the peep-hole open. It was only through this pocket-watch-sized round hole that a little of the musty cellar-air penetrated into the vapour-filled cell. The man shook his head disapprovingly as if I had made an utterly unreasonable request. All the same, he left the lid of the spy-hole open for a considerable time.

Thus, the first day of my long imprisonment ended, one might say, with honours even and, therefore, reassuringly; for not only had I been accused, but I too had accused, even unwittingly shocked someone, and thus identical emotions had created a kind of kinship between myself and another human being. For a long time to come no more such conversations giving rise to arbitrary–and perhaps self-deluding–imaginings were to fall to my lot.

2

To Sleep or Not to Sleep

THE investigators proved to be conservative. They remained true to their truncheons all through the second day. If this time they concentrated on my kidneys, they did not neglect the soles of my feet, for which purpose they repeatedly resorted to the carpet-rolling process. There were six or seven of them taking turns in such a way that there were always four in the room with me.

They must have realized that my purple-blue, swollen soles, as well as the other parts of my body that had been belaboured with the truncheons were, in their maimed condition, incomparably more sensitive than on the first day. One even hinted at this by declaring that increased exertion was superfluous as the truncheon was becoming more and more effective and the pain I suffered more and more unbearable, so that it could be only a question of time, a short time at that, before I would give in and confess to anything including multiple homicide.

I took these allusions to be simply rhetoric; it seemed to me that Szönyi's accusations must really have convinced the investigators that they had caught a spy. However, it seemed somewhat suspicious, even bewildering, that they made no attempt to check even the most easily ascertainable evidence in Szönyi's accusation, that they took no steps to find out whether I had indeed been to see Szönyi or entered Party Headquarters at all at the time in question.

I believed, like hundreds of others, that I was the victim of a 'fatal' error and it never entered my head to admit even part of the false accusation in order to gain temporary, or perhaps even permanent respite from physical torment.

It must have been on the night following the second day that, rolled in the carpet, I at last lost consciousness. By the time I came to, the room was crowded with people, some of whom I knew, some I had never met. Among those I knew, apart from my usual interlocutors, were Dr. Bálint, Chief Physician of the ÁVH, and Colonel Ernö Szücs, Péter's deputy. Dr. Bálint must have given me an injection; soon after I regained consciousness, he disappeared, but Szücs remained sitting on the arm of the easy-chair watching me make vain attempts to rise, only to fall back, dizzy, on the floor. Then he remarked that he, too, had had his soles beaten bloody by the Fascists more than once.

I replied in a low voice that, even according to the Colonel then, there were no essential differences between the present methods and those applied by the Fascists. One of my interrogators raised his truncheon to hit me but Szücs held him back. He stood up, gazed at me for a long time, then asked:

'Do you know Ferenc Vági?'

'I've met Ferenc Vági, the Head of the press department of the Prime Minister's office. Is he the one you mean?'

Szücs nodded, then added:

'I mean him. Only he is no longer press department head, either of the Prime Minister's office or anywhere else because we've arrested him. Do you know Földi, Dobó, Kálmán, Demeter?' The Colonel listed a few more names, looked at me expectantly and said, 'Because we've arrested them too.'

As I learned later, in prison, all the persons mentioned by Szücs had been Hungarian exiles in Switzerland during the Second World War, where, under Szönyi's leadership, they had formed an anti-Hitler group. Most of them I had never met but those I had come across, men like Vági and Kálmán, had appeared to me to be dyed-in-the-wool communists.

Once, when I was still at the Foreign Ministry, I discussed with Vági how many copies of Western newspapers should be allowed to enter the country. At the time, the régime was still boasting that in the streets of Budapest you could buy *The Times* as well as *L'Humanité*, *Le Figaro* as well as the *Daily Worker*, and that not only *L' Unitá* was available but also the *New York Times* and the *Zürcher Zeitung*. Vági had showed every inclination to whittle down the number of copies available to the public to practically nil.

Nor were my recollections of a discussion I had with Kálmán more agreeable. He and I had clashed at a meeting of the ideological seminar-instructors. Rather ironically, perhaps, I had criticized one of the speakers who, with noble simplicity and relentless consistency, kept calling the United States 'Fascist'. I spoke against the constantly multiplying over-simplifications and conceptual mystifications of Party jargon. Well, András Kálmán hastened to the defence of the speaker against my 'unjustified irony', and what is more, went on to express his approval of the terminology that branded the United States as fascist. A few weeks after this event I was informed by the Party group of the Foreign Ministry that I could not be allowed to take part in instructor seminars because, according to the official party organ my views betrayed Trotskyite deviations. Two or three months later, without my having done anything about it, the prohibition was withdrawn.

All this flashed through my mind at the mention of Kálmán's name, and the charge of Trotskyite deviation, which less than a year ago had made me smile, now filled me with unpleasant foreboding. Yet, while sitting on the floor I sought Ernö Szücs's tiny, hardly discoverable eyes in his beefy, red, face, the arrest of these two blinkered Communists seemed to me even more mysterious than my own. Szücs must have misunderstood my glance, or pretended to misunderstand it, for he said:

'So you see, we've rounded up the whole gang. It surprises you, doesn't it? Do you still think it is worth while standing out? Why don't you tell me what kind of letter you brought Szönyi from Wagner?'

My face must have assumed a pretty dumb expression for even the surly Szücs laughed out loud:

'All right,' he said in an almost fatherly tone, 'let's leave it at that for the moment. But you'd better give this matter of the letter some thought.'

Then he drew one of the ÁVH men aside and gave him instructions in a low voice.

Soon two investigators took me under the arms, lifted me from the floor and half-carried me down to the cellar. Later, when Lehota opened the door to hand me a plate of cold, slimy, poppy-seed noodles, I realized that I hadn't eaten since my arrest. Last night they had given me no supper, and today no breakfast, no lunch and no dinner. Yet I returned, almost untouched, the plate on which the noodles, sparingly bestrewn with poppy-seed, lay stiff like worms in *rigor mortis*. Instead of eating, I reflected that in the meantime Szönyi must have supplemented and filled out his story, for Szücs was already demanding from me an account of a fictitious letter.

The discouraging idea that the ÁVH men were giving full credit to Szönyi's fabrication matured into conviction during the promptly resumed hours of manhandling which they carried on till dawn. Again my interrogators behaved like belligerent drunks rather than inquisitors conscientiously plying their trade. They surrounded me in a tight circle in the tower room and assault followed assault like waves breaking on the shore. In the rather infrequent pauses between showers of blows and screamed curses they enquired only about Wagner's letter and seemed to take it as proven that I had been the connecting link between Tibor Szönyi and the mysterious Wagner. From first to last it was obvious that these primitive men, beside themselves with rage, were not shamming—their ingenuity would hardly have run to such good acting—they were firmly convinced that they were dealing with a dangerous, stubborn spy, a determined enemy of the State, who refused to confess out of unwillingness to betray his contact line.

As, to my mind, Szönyi's false accusation largely explained the behaviour of the ÁVH men—officers and investigators alike—I still sought no secret purpose behind the application of means intended to break me physically but believed it was for the sole purpose of uncovering a truly existing espionage ring. In the short pauses between the concentrated attacks I confined myself to reiterating again and again that Szönyi was not telling the truth. I went on repeating this until dawn broke. Then my investigators, seeing that I was unable to leave the tower-room under my own propulsion, dragged me down to the cellar.

A few hours later they handed in some luke-warm slop resembling tea and a thin slice of bread, then, towards noon, they fetched me from my cell. Again I was surrounded by five or six hard-faced men. Lehota hit me in the back, then bandaged my eyes with a damp towel. The iron door of the cellar was flung open and reaching under my arms, two men dragged me up the concrete steps. In the garage they pushed me into a car, its engine already running. We drove to the Andrássy Street headquarters of the ÁVH where I was once again locked in an underground cell.

Compared with the mouse-hole in the cellar of the Buda villa, this cell seemed like a ball-room although it could not have been longer than eight or wider than four feet. The furnishings consisted of a wooden bunk with metal legs embedded in the concrete floor. Above the door of the windowless room, just as in the villa, an electric bulb glowed day and night behind a wire net, throwing its light straight into the eyes of the prisoner lying on the bunk.

Two ÁVH-guards stood at every turn in the labyrinth of cellar corridors, one in civilian clothes with a revolver stuck in his belt and one in uniform with a rifle slung over his shoulder. When a prisoner was being led to an interrogating room, or even to the lavatory, the guards posted at the corners of the corridor signalled to each other with a hiss whether or not the coast was clear, so as to prevent any two prisoners coming face to face. During the eighteen months of my preliminary detention, most of which I spent in this cellar, the rules and regulations of the underground prison, as well as its staff, were frequently changed. The uniformed guards were the first to disappear, then the plain-clothes men either carried no guns or concealed them in their pockets; they also began to wear felt slippers over their shoes to deaden the sound of their approach. In these eighteen months the premises of the ÁVH, below and above ground, were repeatedly rebuilt then changed back to their original condition, but each time they increased the number of interrogation rooms and underground cells, and moved the secret staircase leading from the cellar to the ground-floor and the floors above. But the hissing which served as a signalling system was preserved to the end.

Apart from this hissing, no human sound was audible in the corridors, though they were frenziedly noisy. Instead of the pocket-watch-sized Judas-holes, usual in prisons, there were here six-inch lids on the wooden doors, and hinged iron plates on the metal ones. The guards, making the rounds, would open these lids every eight or ten minutes, particularly at night, then slam them shut with such force that the clanging sounded almost like gun-fire echoing in the catacombs. If any prisoner was not awakened by the sound, the guard would kick his cell-door until the prisoner raised his eyes. Thus, however exhausted the prisoner, he could only doze for a few brief minutes.

The humid cold in the cellar was such that the ÁVH guards wore overcoats or even short fur-lined coats but it was a long time before I was given even a blanket. The food consisted of approximately half a pint of flour-soup in the mornings and around four o'clock in the afternoon, a little over half a pint of beans. With each meal the prisoners were given roughly an ounce and a half of bread. Not once during my first six weeks was the monotony of the diet broken. If, as frequently happened, the prisoner was not crouching shivering in his cell at four o'clock in the afternoon, but was being put through his paces in one of the interrogation rooms, he was deprived of even this cruelly insufficient food.

After the morning soup and the afternoon beans the guards would put the empty dixie-cans outside the cell doors and conduct each prisoner to the lavatory. If a long-standing prisoner, passing the row of cells at such times, noticed left-overs in a dixie, he knew with absolute certainty that a newly arrested person was brooding behind the brown-painted door, unable–as he himself had been at first–to consume even the small quantity of food granted him.

Compared with the atmosphere of the interrogating rooms, the starvation, the cold, the oppressive silence and even the exasperating hissing in the cellar passages seemed restful. At least, that is how I felt every time I was led back, in that first week, from the floors above to my cell. I was now in the hands of the three men who had arrested me. This time, instead of my feet, they hit the palms and the backs of my hands, swinging their truncheons through three-quarters of a circle, or forced me to do squatting exercises until I collapsed with exhaustion. All the while the grey-haired one would read out questions from a slip of paper from which it appeared that they took it as proven, not merely that I was a spy who had established contact between Szönyi and the mysterious Wagner, but also that I had organized an espionage ring when I was at the Foreign Ministry. After one of these periods of physical training lasting two and a half hours–I remember their duration exactly because, in self-defence, I tried ignoring the questions and concentrated my attention on the black-faced wrist-watch of the grey-haired interrogator–when they grew tired of the fruitless baiting and handed me over to an armed guard to take me back to the cellar, I stumbled and jack-knifed over the bannister. The guard dragged me down to my cell where, a few minutes later, the grey-haired man made his appearance and rated me for my alleged attempt at suicide, as though for personal reasons of revenge I had tried to involve him in a painful situation. By the time he had relieved his indignation by striking me across the face, I felt it was superfluous to explain in detail why, exactly, I had collapsed over the bannister. However, from then on, the lid of the Judas-hole was opened more frequently and I was escorted on the stairs by not one, but by two or even three guards.

Early next morning, I was taken to another wing of the building. At the desk facing the door sat a remarkably handsome, characteristically Transdanubian young man, with a black moustache. He eyed me darkly, then, for the first time since my arrest I was offered a seat. He opened a file, leafed through the documents it contained and then declared that I would have to give an exact, detailed account of my life–for the moment, only up to the day when I became an agent of the British or American–it didn't matter which–secret service. I could only repeat that I had never been a member of any secret service, British, American or Russian; all such insinuations were totally unfounded, mere inventions. The young man took a rubber truncheon from the drawer of his desk and rose. He was well over six foot tall, a giant with a splendidly proportioned athletic body. He walked up and down in front of me, then, as if restraining himself, sat down again behind his desk. But the truncheon remained on top of the desk, near his right hand.

For a while he stared at me silently, then he began to speak ponderously, with the accent of the uneducated. And yet, his sentences had a ring agreeable to my ear because the lad spoke the dialect of my county, County Vas in western Hungary.

'Look,' he said, 'we are on to something really big. Some people may get more than they deserve. That's tough. But, you bet your life, the guilty ones will not slip between our fingers. Our people's democracy is still too young; it cannot afford such luxuries. Look, I am a worker . . .'

While he paused for breath, I added in a low voice:

'From County Vas, at that . . .'

'How do you know? Or rather, what gave you the idea?' he corrected himself guiltily, retracting his confirmation of my guess.

'I can hear it. You probably come from the eastern part of the County.'

The giant looked at me dumbfounded, because ÁVH officers were always careful to conceal their identity and, when necessary, used cover names before their prisoners.

'You know a lot,' he remarked, 'too much. Still, it seems that there are things even you don't understand. So let me enlighten you by telling you a little story. It happened in the Soviet Union . . .'

As if reciting a well-prepared text, the giant related how at some undefined time, in some undefined place, an act of sabotage had been committed in the Soviet Union. Three people were suspected, none of whom would confess to the crime. What was to be done? All three suspects had to be executed. Regrettably. But a socialist state surrounded by hostile capitalist powers, cannot afford to let a saboteur go unpunished. So, the young man from County Vas concluded, hitting the desk with his truncheon for added emphasis, I should not imagine for a moment that my obstinate denials would save me from the scaffold. The only way in which I could help myself was to repent and admit my guilt.

I had no wish to quote another Russian example, Dostoevsky, and repeat the story of Christ and the Grand Inquisitor. I couldn't have done so even had I wished, because at that moment the overfed, brutal-faced ÁVH man who had participated in my arrest, entered the room. He sat down without a word and opened a large envelope addressed in a rather awkward female hand to 'Comrade Vajda'. Whether this was his real name or not, from then on this vulgar featured young man was Vajda to me. He tore open the envelope, perused the contents with great attention, then locked them away in his desk. In the meantime the lad from County Vas began to unwind the thread of my life.

First came my family. When I readily acknowledged that my father had been General Manager of the Electricity Works of County Vas, the two men exchanged meaningful glances, then they delved with gusto into my mother's background, with special emphasis on the army officers in her family. From their attitude one might have thought the mere fact that four of my cousins had chosen the army as a career—two as long ago as the days of the Austro-Hungarian monarchy—was in itself unequivocal proof in support of Szönyi's allegations. They commented in the same way on the Catholic private school I had attended, the once famous University College where I studied in Budapest and my two terms at the Sorbonne. Vajda remarked darkly that even in the absence of other information, it was obvious to him that someone brought up in such an environment could never have joined the then illegal communist party in good faith. Fortunately, there was sufficient evidence to show that in my university days, in 1932, I had wormed my way into the communist movement on behalf of Horthy's political police as an *agent provocateur*. It would be better for me if I told them of my own free will how I began and how I carried on my activities as a police spy before they were forced to confront me with the information at their disposal.

When I expressed doubts as to the ÁVH or anyone else being able to prove something that never took place, they reached for their rubber truncheons. After some preliminary skirmishing they pressed my forehead against the uneven gritty wall. They ordered me to keep my hands along the seams of my trousers and hold my body stiff as a poker so that it formed one side of a right-angled triangle between the wall and the floor. They took off my shoes to prevent me from slipping. The handsome lad from my county squatted down near me and beat my toes with his truncheon. It was not long before the right-angled triangle, of which my body was the hypotenuse, collapsed. But my interrogators soon restored me to the classic geometrical form. Still, this ingenious innovation that would have amazed Euclid, did not prevent the couple from indulging in the usual pranks: the kidney-blows, the palm-rapping, with 180° swings of the truncheon, and the bastinados. This time they did not

25

use a carpet for the performance. Not only because there were no such luxuries in the bare interrogation room, but also because my weakened physical condition rendered such props unnecessary.

A few days later, at dawn, after a less violent night than usual, Vajda sat down to the typewriter to draft my first statement. They required only a few ordinary facts: date of birth, the schools I attended, my visit to Paris in 1937 and from there, in 1939, to the Argentine; my return to Budapest in 1946. After the first sentences we reached a deadlock, for Vajda wrote, 'In 1937 I went to Paris to seek adventure.'

I insisted that I had gone to Paris not to seek adventure but to study, so he had better delete that part of the sentence or I would not be in a position to sign the statement. It may have been utterly unreasonable to dig in my heels because of this mildly pejorative sentence but somehow I felt that if I gave in at this point, if I once started to slide down the slope of submissiveness, I might go all the way and would soon admit not only that I had established contact between Wagner and Szönyi, not only that I had created an espionage ring in the Foreign Ministry, but also that in early youth I had set out on my political and moral career as a police spy.

Vajda jumped up from his chair in fury and, joined by the youth from County Vas, was reaching for his instrument of persuasion, the truncheon, when the door flew open to admit two plain-clothes security men and a uniformed guard with a rifle on his shoulder. The two civilians conducted a whispered conversation with my interrogators, then led me away. Glancing back, I saw Vajda tear the paper from the typewriter, crush it in his hand and fling it into the waste-paper basket.

We walked through an intricate system of corridors until, at last, we entered a pleasantly furnished study. A man with thinning reddish-blond hair and the mild face of a priest sat behind the desk. He wore gold-rimmed glasses and his blinking, myopic eyes gave his features an expression of cunning. His smile was almost friendly as he pointed to the armchair facing the desk and motioned me to sit down. When we were alone he yawned deeply, removed his spectacles, rubbed his eyes, then leaned back in his armchair, visibly exhausted; a few minutes later he placed his elbows on top of the desk and addressed me:

'Well,' he began, placing the glasses back on his nose, 'how do you feel?'

TO SLEEP OR NOT TO SLEEP

I shrugged my shoulders.

'That black ring round your eye looks quite amusing. What was it, a boxing match?'

Ignoring this question, I declared that in my opinion we could get at the truth much quicker if the ÁVH relied on facts, not on slander, and if, before accusing someone, they took the trouble to check verifiable information, as, for example, Tibor Szönyi's deposition. The man with the glasses laughed ambiguously:

'Forget Szönyi,' he said, waving his hand. 'We are concerned with something entirely different. Szönyi is a side-issue, so are you. Do you smoke? Do you want a cup of tea? With lemon?'

I accepted the cigarette. The priestly-faced individual rang the bell. An attractive secretary came in. She listened to his instructions in silence and after a short while returned with a cup of lemon tea and a piece of cake which she put down before me. During her absence we sat in utter silence. The bespectacled man rose from behind his desk and threw himself, with an air of great weariness, into a deep armchair. He was of medium height, thicker around the waist than his age warranted. Later, I was to see that pink face, those blunt-fingered, soft hands, often enough. His name was Mátyás Károlyi, and although at the time he was only a major, he belonged to Gábor Péter's inner circle. This inner, or to use the ÁVH name for it, conspiratorial circle, directed the most secret activities of the political police. Its members were selected by Gábor Péter person-ally; they were not chosen according to rank but from his most loyal followers that he considered best fitted for the job. Thus it frequently happened that a lieutenant, drawn into the conspiratorial circle, wielded far greater power than many a major or lieutenant-colonel. A member of the inner circle could at times even give orders to his superiors.

When the secretary had quietly closed the door behind her, Károlyi scrambled to his feet and went back to his desk.

'Drink your tea first,' he said, staring at me short-sightedly. Then, unexpectedly, he asked:

'When did you first meet László Rajk?'

I did not attach great importance to the question, believing it to be of an introductory nature. I replied off-handedly:

'At the University. We were there together. I think we met for the first time around 1930.'

'Did you know that Rajk was a police spy?'

I glanced at Károlyi quickly—the suspicion flashed into my mind that he was laying a trap for me for some obscure purpose of his own.

After all, László Rajk was looked upon as the top man among the communist leaders, neither trained in Russia nor sent home by Moscow. Already in 1945 his past in the underground communist movement, his role in the Hungarian Brigade fighting in the Spanish civil war, and his activities in the Hungarian Resistance movement during the German occupation had won him such prestige that he was entrusted with the most important portfolio, that of Minister of the Interior, and in 1948 was appointed Minister of Foreign Affairs. When László Rajk took over Foreign Affairs, and the moderately gifted János Kádár was made Minister of the Interior, the communists in the know did not regard Rajk as demoted. On the contrary, they thought that consolidation in the country had reached a point where it was no longer important to have anyone as outstanding as Rajk to deal with domestic affairs; instead of presuming that Rajk had lost prestige by becoming Foreign Minister, they believed that the Party leadership had delegated Rajk to this post because foreign policy had increased in importance.

This was the line that Mátyás Rákosi took in the narrower circle of the leadership, but it may well be that even he was as yet unaware of the fate awaiting Rajk. This supposition seems confirmed by a telephone conversation between Rákosi and one of the leading officials of the Foreign Ministry. Shortly before Rajk's appointment, Rákosi telephoned Dr. György Heltai, head of the Foreign Ministry's political department.

'Well, have you heard the great news?' he asked Heltai.

There had been rumours that Erik Molnár was to be replaced by László Rajk, and Heltai replied truthfully that he had heard whispers of certain impending changes. Rákosi then informed him squarely that Rajk would be the new Foreign Minister and added, by way of explanation:

'The Foreign Ministry has been a Kindergarten long enough. Now you will have an adult to lead you.'

The word *kindergarten* was an ironic reference to the activities and attitude of the departing Foreign Minister, Erik Molnár. Molnár, although he had been a member of the Communist Party for several decades, had never been to Moscow. He had participated in the underground communist movement not so much as a militant as by contributing historical and agrarian-political essays to crypto-communist periodicals. His brother, René Molnár, however, who had acted for a considerable time as defence counsel for the imprisoned communists in Budapest and was later compelled to flee to Moscow, had there fallen victim to the 1937 Trotsky trials.

Whether this was the reason, or whether the administration of the Foreign Ministry held but limited interest for Molnár, he was careful to avoid taking any independent action or of forming decisions. Even on the most insignificant questions, he would turn for instruction or advice to Party headquarters or the Soviet authorities. It often happened that Molnár would interrupt the usual reports of the departmental heads and in their presence–and often in mine–would ring up Rákosi, Révai, or the Soviet Ambassador, Pushkin, on the secret, so-called 'chaika' line, before informing us of his decision. In the middle drawer of his desk he kept books to read during office hours. If anyone entered his room, he hastily shut the drawer, his face wearing the expression of a schoolboy caught using a crib.

Thus, not only Rákosi regarded Rajk, Molnár's junior by a good many years, as more 'adult', but so did everyone who placed more value on a practical politician than on a scholar of theoretical bent. Although it was no secret among the well-informed that Rajk had suffered some loss of prestige when the Politbureau of the Communist Party had sharply criticized his views concerning the role of the party group within the Ministry of the Interior–criticism followed by his transfer to the Foreign Ministry–no particular significance was attached to the affair in 1948, for in the course of that year which Rákosi called 'the year of change', the entire state administration was undergoing large-scale reorganization.

The trend of the changes taking place became increasingly clear. When, at the end of 1948, I was transferred from the Foreign Ministry, where I was deputy head of the press and information department, to the Ministry of Agriculture to head the press department there, many of the old officials, even those appointed after 1945, were recalled from their diplomatic posts abroad or discharged from their jobs, and replaced in the Ministries as at the Embassies by party functionaries of working-class origin or, even more frequently, by men from the ÁVH. The salaries of those who had been in the secret police were usually supplemented from ÁVH funds. Among these, for example, was ÁVH-Major Tamás Mátrai, appointed, in the summer of 1948, ministerial counsellor at the Ministry of Foreign Affairs. Mátrai's salary at the Ministry amounted to approximately 900 forints but at the same time he drew an additional 1500 forints from ÁVH funds. He once rang them up in my presence, to demand a remittance.

In the course of the reorganization of the Foreign Ministry, Mátrai built up a so-called administrative department with himself as its head. This department did no more than perform the duties of

two consular officials but Mátrai inflated it into a powerful bureau-
cratic control organization. He took over the issuing of diplomatic
passports that had, until then, been outside the jurisdiction of the
secret police, assumed direction of the courier service in order to be
able to use the diplomatic bag, and so take advantage both of the
passports and the bag for the purposes of the ÁVH. At the same
time, his department, on the pretext of administrative reorganization,
sought to bring every department of the Foreign Ministry under
police surveillance.

Years later, from hints dropped in prison, I gathered that even
then the Minister of Foreign Affairs himself had long been under
surveillance. The principal *commissar*, however, did not report to
Gábor Péter, like Mátrai, but in all probability directly to the
Russians and took his instructions from them. This *commissar* was
the Muscovite, Andor Berei, who became Undersecretary of Foreign
Affairs in 1948, when Rajk took over the Foreign Ministry.

Between the two world wars, Berei had functioned as a so-called
'instructor' in the Communist International and as the Comintern's
trusted emissary had assisted in the foundation and running of the
Belgian Communist Party. These Comintern instructors were
almost without exception representatives not only of the Comintern
but also of the Soviet secret police, the NKVD. Berei's erudition,
broad intellectual horizon and quick mind raised him above his
fellow-instructors. Perhaps it was because of these qualities – considered highly suspect in Moscow – that, though he had always been a
conformist, he never rose to the front rank. The most he achieved
was to act as prompter to less discerning people, persons without
stature, who could never be suspected of conceiving, by any un-
fortunate mischance, ideas of their own.

It was obvious from the first that the Foreign Ministry held
as little interest for Berei as it did for Molnár. Berei's loyalties were
still with the National Planning Bureau of which, before his appointment as Undersecretary of Foreign Affairs, he had been head. But
former instructor Berei of the Comintern could hardly have been
acting on his own initiative when he issued orders behind Rajk's
back, countermanded the Minister's instructions and took charge of
affairs in which only the Minister himself should have had powers of
decision. This – as I later learned – had caused several clashes between
Rajk and Berei in March and April, 1949. At the time of my interrogation, I was still unaware of these behind-the-scene conflicts as I

had spent the last few months before my arrest at the Ministry of Agriculture. But I recalled all the more clearly the May-Day celebrations when, standing on a rostrum in front of the gala-tribune next to the Party's first secretary, Mátyás Rákosi, Foreign Minister László Rajk greeted the demonstrators.

This scene had imprinted itself on my mind because, side by side with the tall, handsome, slender Rajk, the squat and neckless Rákosi had cut a ludicrous figure as, with his hat pulled down over his ears, he stood red and sweating in the sunshine. Rákosi was always very careful lest the contrast between himself and others should increase the aversion inspired by his unprepossessing appearance. If, in spite of this, he had invited Rajk to stand at his side, this meant in the flower-language of Party protocol that next to Rákosi, Rajk counted as one of the foremost leaders of the Party. What then, I wondered, was the purpose of the interrogator's leading question?–'Do you know that Rajk was a police spy under Horthy?' After a while Károlyi grew tired of my silence.

'Answer me! Did you know that Rajk was a police spy?'

'In my opinion that is utterly impossible,' I replied.

Károlyi broke into loud and long false police-laughter.

'Of course!' he cried, 'the two buddies protect one another. I hope you realize that this makes you look even more suspicious?'

I was about to speak but he silenced me.

'I know, I know. Szönyi is lying. But in the face of his and other similar confessions, your denials won't be worth much. That's obvious, isn't it? However, if you agree to help me, I may be able to help you too.'

'What do you mean by helping?' I asked suspiciously. 'I cannot testify that Rajk was a police spy.'

'We don't require that from you. All you have to do is tell the truth. Isn't it true that in 1931 you were one of the initiators of the communist student-movement?'

I nodded.

'When did you come to Budapest?'

'In 1928, after I left school.'

'And you enrolled in the Faculty of Letters?'

'No. First in the Faculty of Foreign Affairs of the School of Economics.'

'In short, you were one of the privileged. You were raised in a hot-house where they nurtured the diplomatic shoots of the Horthy régime.' Károlyi, who was about the same age as myself, and was, therefore, familiar with conditions in those days, smiled ironically.

31

'How did you come to be a communist? At that time, the party was still underground!'

Yes, it was at that time the party had gone underground and the universities were ruled by right-wing student organizations called *fraternal societies*. Their members wore flat, visored caps—each faculty and organization a different colour—and participated in para-military manoeuvres and demonstrations. They received semi-official support from the government and were given preference among those applying for state scholarships. The patrons of the *fraternal societies*, so-called *domini* (usually outstanding right-wing public figures) lent them a helping hand after graduation. With an energy worthy of free-mason solidarity these patrons threw their weight into the scale when it came to finding jobs for these young men 'reliable from the point of view of national loyalty'. They were promised rapid advancement in the state administration or with the more important private enterprises. Neither the semi-official mentors nor the *domini* objected on moral grounds—though they did not relish the reaction abroad—when at the beginning of the academic year, the *fraternal societies* launched noisy and brutal 'Jew-beatings' in the otherwise sleepy and uninspired halls of science, to scare off the Jewish students already admitted in limited numbers to the universities.

To politically-minded young people who viewed the rule of the *fraternal societies* in the universities with deep revulsion, and who were driven into sharp opposition to the *fraternal societies* and their patron, the Horthy régime, the perhaps realistic but cautious opposition of the other parties including the Social Democrats seemed luke-warm and opportunistic. They wanted something more radical. Particularly those who, like myself, went on lonely walks of exploration at night in the streets of the capital and looked around with a feeling of guilt at the slums of Budapest, because they blamed their families, and even themselves, for what they saw. So after a year, I left the Faculty of Diplomacy, left the College with its white-gloved footmen, took a room in town and enrolled at the University. I became an habitué of the literary cafés, made friends with left-wing writers, wrote poems, essays and short stories, and edited, in company with other young writers, a number of short-lived literary periodicals. I joined the Jaurès-circle, contributed to left-wing publications appearing abroad, dug deep into Marxist literature, and then enrolled for a term at the Sorbonne.

Of all this I told Károlyi only that I had spent two terms at the Sorbonne in 1930, made friends with French communist students and on returning home, had sought contact with the underground Hungarian Communist Party. To further questions I answered that at first I took part in the activities of the so-called party 'apparatus'. I carried typewriters, stencils and printing ink to illegal printing shops, acted as courier and contact man and, at the same time, had instructions to keep my eyes open at the university and form a communist cell with the students sympathetic to our cause. The first man I won over for the movement was István Stolte, who had been a class-mate of mine for ten years, right through primary and secondary school, and whose thinking ran along the same lines as mine.

'We have now come to Stolte,' Károlyi nodded, then he offered me another cigarette.

'And Rajk?'

Rajk was a tall, slender, very masculine-looking youth. With his inordinately high forehead, protruding cheekbones, sharply-drawn features, he bore an astounding resemblance—as American newspapermen remarked later, when he was Foreign Minister – to Abraham Lincoln, and from the Foreign Minister's *curriculum vitae*, the journalists learnt that he was born exactly 100 years after the American President. This chance parallel was, of course, never referred to in the corridors of the Budapest University, but Rajk's bright eyes, his radiant, charming smile and calm, unhurried way of speaking inspired confidence among fellow students of the most varied backgrounds and intellectual levels.

'Well, and Rajk?' Károlyi repeated impatiently.

'Stolte drew my attention to the fact that László Rajk's attitude was similar to ours.'

'So you recruited him for the movement?'

'No. Until then my relations with Rajk had been only superficial, though friendly. So I approached him with caution. All the more so as I had strict instructions to be careful that no-one at the University should suspect me of being a communist; should I arouse suspicion, I would endanger my immediate contacts as well as the underground network attached to me.'

'What was the subject of your first conversation with Rajk?'

'We talked mainly about our studies. It was only gradually that we shifted to sociological and political subjects.'

'Didn't Rajk introduce his friends to you?'

'He did. Rajk was a member of a small circle formed around a fellow student called Mészáros. This circle read and discussed sociological, mainly Marxist works. Mészáros held that it was sense-less to join any kind of movement or party, to say nothing of exposing oneself to the dangers of illegality, before one had a thorough insight into the theoretical side of it.'

'Did Rajk approve of this attitude?'

'My impression was that though Rajk regarded this attitude as sensible, his practical turn of mind as well as his temperament were driving him, like most young men, towards action. I felt that I had to let him make his own choice and so I made no attempt to persuade Rajk to join us in our first action.'

'What was your first action?'

'We distributed leaflets at the College of Technical Sciences, the Faculty of Letters and a few student hostels. On the same day the yellow press announced this small incident in huge headlines, proclaiming that the communists had infiltrated into the universities. The régime, convinced as it was that it had the students under its thumb, partly through the *fraternal societies*, partly because of the thorough screening before admission, was in a flaming rage.'

'And then? Was anyone arrested?'

'No-one. But next day the corridors were crawling with secret police. A couple of us took their presence as a challenge and, behind the backs of the preposterous, stupid, bowler-hatted detectives, we stuffed leaflets into the desks in the empty classrooms and in the window-recesses before lectures began.'

'We don't wear bowler hats,' Károlyi remarked, feeling perhaps that my scorn was addressed not only to the secret police of the past; then he added significantly, 'And we're not stupid, either. Now give me a detailed account of what happened next, and also when you met Rajk again and how and by whom he was recruited into the movement.'

I tried to sum up my recollections of the next few days. 'Yes, the members of the *fraternal societies* made everyone entering the building identify themselves; only students were admitted. After the second distribution of leaflets it thus became evident that the theory advanced by some of the newspapers–that the leaflets had been smuggled in by an outsider–could not be true. The *fraternal societies* organized search parties for several days in succession. They combed the classes and in order to prove that the student body they led along the path of loyalty to the nation could not be responsible for the leaflets, they handed over to the police a few innocent elderly scholars who came to attend Professor Gerevich's lectures on the history of art. False rumours spread and, at times, the corridors were more crowded than the class-rooms. It was in this atmosphere that I met Rajk again.

'Even today I don't know whether or not he had guessed that I had had something to do with the events of those days, but it is certain that he asked no questions and we mentioned neither the leaflets nor the articles appearing in the press, nor the alarms and excursions of the flat-caps. As far as I can remember we were talking about a recently published essay on the French revolution. We were walking up and down the corridor when the warning bell before lectures interrupted our conversation. Rajk stopped short, spoke my name, then added without any preamble:

' ". . . there is only one solution: Lenin."

'We entered the class-room but did not sit together. The next day I told Stolte to contact Rajk openly, in the name of the communist student group.'

'So it is absolutely clear that it was Stolte who recruited Rajk for the party?'

'There can be no doubt of it. I myself instructed him to do so.'

'Are you ready to repeat this to Rajk's face?'

'Why? Does he deny it?'

'It is not for you to ask questions,' the major declared coldly. 'Are you, or are you not ready to say this to his face?'

'It is true. Therefore I am ready.'

'All right,' Károlyi nodded, 'let's get on then. How did the student movement develop?'

I described how the movement took shape. Stolte formed another group at the Eötvös College which was considered a significant success because this college, modelled on the French École Normale Supérieure, drew unchallenged upon the intellectual élite, students whose voices were listened to by others. Later, I was instructed to establish contact between Stolte and the league of young communist workers, and then to withdraw from the university movement because the work I would have to do in the rural department of the party—to which I was being transferred—ruled out a doubling of jobs that might prove dangerous from the conspiratorial point of view. Thus, Stolte became secretary of the University group, but my friends kept me informed concerning the development of the student movement.

'And what happened to you?'

'I was arrested in 1932, together with the leaders of the rural section.'

'Did you continue to obtain information concerning the activities of the student group?'

'Yes. My friends outwitted the censors by sending me books in which certain letters had pin-point marks under them. From these letters I could decipher their message.'

'You don't say!' Károlyi exclaimed laughing. 'Changed days!' Then he became serious again.

'And when did Stolte become a Trotskyite and police spy?'

'As far as I know Stolte's party membership was suspended in 1933, after the arrest of the University group. I think I am right in saying that was when Rajk was appointed secretary of the student movement. Later, Stolte was expelled from the party as a Trotskyite and police agent.'

'And Rajk continued to maintain contact with this Trotskyite police spy. Didn't he?'

'My information is that when Stolte was merely a suspended party member and was working on an historical essay, the party instructed Rajk to read and review Stolte's work, partly in his capacity of secretary of the University group, partly as a historian.'

'Did you meet Stolte in those days?'

'I did.'

'You must have been wonderful communists, both of you, to maintain friendly terms with such a suspicious character. Naturally, Rajk went on seeing him even after he had been expelled from the party?'

'I have no idea.'

Károlyi grinned. 'You will. You'll tell us a great deal more about this. Well, for the time being, write down in detail about your meeting with Rajk, your conversation. Mention who recruited Rajk for the underground movement, when and how. That's all for the moment. Do you want a cigarette?'

Károlyi struggled heavily to his feet, made me sit at a small table and put paper, pencil and a few cigarettes in front of me. Then he summoned the guard.

'I'm not giving you any matches', he called back from the door, 'if you want to smoke, ask the comrade for a light. And report to him when you have finished.'

He left the room and I smoked a cigarette. Only then did I begin to wonder about the possible implications of our conversation. In the meantime, however, coolly and objectively, I set down my recollections.

36

Late the following night, two ÁVH guards came to my cell to fetch me and took me to an office much more elegantly furnished than Károlyi's. Here Ernö Szücs received me. He was nervous, tired, impatient. After a few questions about the student movement, he wanted me to tell him who established contact between Rajk and the league of young communist workers. He sat down at his typewriter and drafted a brief statement merely saying that it was Stolte who recruited Rajk to the movement. He asked me whether I would maintain my allegation if I were confronted with Rajk. I said 'Yes, of course I would.'

I was led back to my cell, but soon they fetched me again, shackled me and made me get into a curtained car, standing in the courtyard. I was flanked on both sides by ÁVH men. Even though the curtains completely shut out the world, they placed on my nose a pair of sunglasses, carefully lined with black paper. We must have travelled the same road we had travelled before, we were driven into the same garage and I was dragged down the same steps to the cellar, for, when they took off my glasses, I found myself in the identical cell where I had spent my first day of captivity. After a few minutes in this damp hole, the door opened and I was led up to the first floor. A moment later I was again in the large room I had been in on my first afternoon. Now as before, the head of the T-shaped table was occupied by Gábor Péter and his general staff. But, standing at the foot of the T, slightly to my right, was László Rajk. They pushed me somewhat to the left, so that I was facing him.

On the table in front of Rajk lay several sheets of paper and he was holding a sharpened pencil in his hand. He wore neither jacket, nor tie, his shirt hung crumpled, half-unbuttoned, his medium-grey trousers–he wore no belt–had slipped down below his waist. His usually rugged but now ashen face was turned towards me but his eyes, gazing at me, were sightless. The lines on his forehead had deepened into hard hollows and three straight parallel furrows marred his exhausted face, as if drawn with a ruler. No-one except the interrogators and their superiors will ever know what Rajk went through during this first period of his imprisonment; it is still a mystery to me what could have caused the three parallel furrows searing his face.

Years later, comparing dates, I came to the conclusion that the day of our confrontation must have been Rajk's third day in the hands of the ÁVH. Three days before, late in the evening, he had been sitting talking to his wife, watching her feed their little son László, then a few weeks old, when Julia Rajk's mother came into the room to tell them that Gábor Péter's men had come to see László. The ÁVH officers were waiting in the hall. Rajk invited the unexpected guests, who had arrived at such an unusual hour, into his study, but one of the officers said brusquely that the nature of what Gábor Péter wanted to discuss with the Minister made it necessary for him to accompany them to headquarters. Rajk protested (he had already heard of my disappearance). Finally, Gábor Péter's men seized him and dragged him away by force. From the window, Julia Rajk watched her husband, still resisting, being pushed feet first, into the waiting black car.

Standing there at the foot of the T-shaped table, staring at my former university colleague, I gave not a thought to our grotesque situation, nor to what lay in store for us. My attention was concentrated on the three horizontal furrows that disfigured him. I was obsessed with the idea that Rajk's face would disintegrate. When Gábor Péter shouted my name, I turned my eyes away from Rajk's face and looked at Péter. Stressing every word, the head of the secret police now asked me:

'Who recruited László Rajk for the party, and who established contact between him and the young workers' movement?'

'István Stolte,' I replied.

'Say it to his face.'

Rajk's eyes strayed across the room as I repeated my statement.

'László Rajk! Do you admit it?'

Rajk flung the pencil he held in his right hand on to the blank sheets of paper lying on the table and said in a low voice:

'I maintain that it was Mészáros.'

'Do you maintain that it was Stolte?' Gábor Péter asked me.

'I do.'

I was led away and at daybreak was taken back to the cellar at 60 Andrássy Street.

Although no-one spoke to me during the day that followed, although I was not taken up for questioning, I found no peace. Could I possibly be mistaken? Was it conceivable that Mészáros had only been pretending to keep himself and his group aloof from the communist movement, and was it dissimulation when he preached the priority of theory and seemingly avoided practical action? Had I falsely accused Rajk at the foot of the T-shaped table where Szönyi had falsely accused me ten days before? For a long time I was unable to rid myself of these doubts although there were many arguments against them. It was not impossible that Mészáros should have had some vague connection with the party that my section knew nothing about, but as far as I knew, Mészáros had stuck to his convictions to the end and refused to participate in any kind of underground organization; what is more, when most members of his group had already joined the student movement his closest friends were still trying in vain to win his co-operation. Thus, both psychologically and organizationally it seemed entirely impossible that Mészáros could have established contact between Rajk and the party, even had he wanted to. Still, the faint chance that I had been mistaken tormented me for years, and therefore, both while in prison and afterwards, I did my utmost to check my recollections, which were later confirmed as true by other prisoners.

But even if Rajk did have some contact with the communist movement through Mészáros, why should he deny his connection with Stolte—something I myself had arranged? This denial awakened my suspicion of the former Foreign Minister, all the more so as its motives appeared obvious.

To be branded a Trotskyite in the Communist Party was equivalent to excommunication and, to the mind of a loyal party-member, Trotskyism seemed as dangerous an infection as did the plague to our mediaeval ancestors. Very often, those repudiated as Trotskyites had not even read Trotsky's works, and had they been familiar with his ideas they would certainly not have sympathized with them. Often their only crime was that they did not unconditionally approve of Moscow's tortuous political line or—like myself in the party organization of the state administration—criticized or made ironical comments on the widespread Stalinist jargon. But Stolte was an authentic Trotskyite. One of the most authentic in Hungary. After his expulsion from the party, he organized a small Trotskyite group, and as its leader, established contact with the regional Trotskyite centre set up by Sedov, Trotsky's son, in Bratislava.

It was therefore clear that László Rajk considered it dangerous to admit his connection with Stolte. No doubt he was more familiar than I with the methods and protocol of the ÁVH. He must have realized that his words would fall on deaf ears if he tried to explain that when he was secretary of the student movement, Stolte was not a Trotskyite and that it was only years later that he established his opposition group. By then Rajk must have known that this negligible difference in time would be completely ignored by the dialectics of the secret police and, regardless of the preposterous nature of such an interpretation, the final statement would contain words to the effect that Rajk had been recruited into the Communist Party by a man expelled as a Trotskyite and Horthy police agent; and this was proof, according to ÁVH logic, that Rajk also must have been a Trotskyite and police agent.

But to my eyes, it was not the connection between the twenty-year-old Stolte, and the twenty-one-year-old Rajk that compromised the former Minister but the fact that he denied that connection. As it was impossible that he should have forgotten this decisive moment of his life—for it was then that he set out with admirable consistency on his career as a professional revolutionary—I believed that Rajk had some ulterior motive for denying the facts. Szönyi must also have been driven by some malicious intention—I argued—when he insisted that his lie was the truth, and, as the behaviour of both gave ample grounds for suspicion, the ÁVH must have had something concrete to go on when they started their investigation.

The accusation made by the head of the cadres department had, objectively, put a rope around my neck, and the suspicion aroused in me by Rajk's denial of facts known to me put me subjectively into an ambivalent frame of mind. I had now found an explanation for the methods of my interrogators in their attempts to unmask spies. I thought that I had no right to draw general and final conclusions from my own experiences as long as I had no way of determining to what extent these brutalities were inspired by genuine indignation or momentary police hysteria.

My relatively abstract reflections were not interrupted until evening when I was again taken up for questioning. During the days that followed the groups of interrogators were frequently changed, though the questions and methods remained unchanged. Only one exception occurred. One night I was led into a very large room. The young man behind the desk made me stand straight, facing him, turned a reflector lamp full into my eyes and began to speak in calm, almost conversational tones. Behind him, to the right, a woman sat at her typewriter in semi-darkness as if she were waiting for dictation. Her face was turned towards me but in the blinding light I could not make out her features, only the shape of her head, hair and shoulders.

The young man began by saying that to him I was obviously not a spy in the generally accepted sense of the word. I belonged to a species he would call communists of Western orientation. His cultured selection of words, his intelligent, well-rounded sentences and civilized voice formed a surprising contrast to the manner of my previous interrogators. He did not ask questions, he lectured.

He argued that those who had returned to Hungary from the so-called bourgeois democracies had brought with them an alien and dangerously destructive mentality, an ingrained prejudice. In the Western countries where, like myself, they had often spent many years, they had attended universities, formed friendships, and so became deeply attached to the West.

He did not doubt that we sincerely regarded ourselves as communists; however, in truly socialist countries we constituted a harmful element, a foreign body. Perhaps unconsciously so. All I had to do was look back over the two and a half years since my return, at the period spent at the Foreign Ministry, and more especially at my term at the Ministry of Agriculture . . .

I replied that I should be grateful if he would be good enough to inform me what incorrectness or act of disloyalty I had committed. The young man laughed.

'Incorrectness and act of disloyalty? You see, this very question justifies me. Just think how destructive you are with these bourgeois notions of yours, your bourgeois scruples and prejudices. Think, man! Think and remember . . .'

While my interrogator elaborated his theme in several variations I tried to steal a glance round the reflector and make out the face of the woman behind the typewriter, for her contours seemed familiar. But all the while I thought and remembered. I recalled particularly something that took place in the middle of March that had really annoyed me at the time. Some party functionary by the name of Baráti, whom I knew only slightly, summoned me one day to Party Headquarters. After a few preliminary sentences he came to the point, saying with friendly directness:

'We want you to issue a communiqué stating that the *kulaks* (the rich farmers) are sabotaging the sowing-plan in the northern counties.'

I explained to him at some length that there was no question of sabotage. The press section of the Ministry of Agriculture had about one thousand agricultural correspondents throughout the country who sent in expert reports on weather conditions, the possibilities and progress of work in the fields and harvest expectations. These reports, which I had carefully studied, unanimously stated that in the northern counties the soil was frozen and in many places covered in snow. In such conditions the Hungarian peasant does not plough, he waits for a thaw—and this was expected within a few days. But even if there were signs of sabotage, of which there were not, I should hesitate to issue such a communiqué which, as it would be published in every newspaper in the country, would cause unnecessary alarm.

Baráti raised his hand. 'You don't think politically, comrade. According to the sowing-plan, ploughing should have been finished by the middle of March and in the northern counties the *kulaks* have failed to accomplish the plan.'

'Any communique,' I had replied, 'could, in all honesty, blame only the weather for the delay.'

Baráti had shrugged his shoulders, and declared that in his opinion I was misjudging, even underestimating, the significance of the struggle against the *kulaks*. For my part I produced new facts in support of my contention that the sabotage charge was purely fictitious. I emphasized, hoping that this practical reasoning would carry more weight, that the communiqué they wanted me to issue would discredit not the accused but the accusers, and in addition might be used as a pretext for acts of personal revenge, violence and manhunts. I had no intention of supplying such a pretext and, I hoped, neither had he.

After we had both argued hotly and for a long time, Baráti pronounced the words that had now brought him to mind, the exact words used by the young ÁVH officer:

'You are a man full of scruples and prejudices, comrade,' he said, looking me up and down reflectively.

I rose and with all the calm I could muster, replied in a low voice:

'That is quite possible. However, as long as I am head of the press section of the Ministry of Agriculture no such communiqués will be issued.'

I was convinced that it was I, not Baráti, who represented the political interests of the Communist Party and protected its moral values. I believed that I had been appointed to the position I held, not to function as an automaton directed by the pushing of various buttons, but to perform my work responsibly, conscientiously, and in the way I thought right.

Still, I was beginning to be discouraged by criticism and misunderstandings and so I had already taken steps to exchange my political post for a desk in a scientific or semi-scientific institute, removed from everyday politics. I felt I had a right to this decision, to this withdrawal. One or two of my old friends might grumble and shake their heads disapprovingly, but the hide-bound, narrow-minded party functionaries would eventually, without my help, fall through the sieve of time.

The phraseology of the party functionary and that of the ÁVH officer bore evidence of such close kinship that I should not have been surprised had the young man orating behind his desk called me to account for the communiqué I had refused to issue. But he mentioned no concrete facts, he was content to enlighten me with generalities.

'The communists of Western orientation,' he continued, 'destructive as they are, however unwittingly, must realize that the Party has to defend itself against them. Though they may not be saboteurs and spies in the military sense, their bourgeois mentality supplies more grist to the enemy's mill than the saboteur who works in a factory or blows up bridges. Thus, these men infected by the West are, in essence,' and he stressed the words *in essence*, 'saboteurs, diversionists and spies, and the Party has no choice but to remove them, especially if they are in high positions, to prevent them spreading the contagion.

'As far as I am concerned,' he declared, 'I am sorry for you when I think what is waiting for you.'

Then, raising his voice, he described in vivid detail how we prisoners would grow old, go off our heads and rot away in our lonely cells while the People's Democracy advanced towards unprecedented prosperity. Suddenly, one of his cleverly turned phrases was interrupted by a loud, sobbing sound. The girl behind the typewriter jumped up from her chair and ran out of the room. Unfortunately, I was unable to see her face.

We could alleviate our lot only, the young man continued unperturbed, by telling sincerely and openly everything we knew, or even suspected, of our acquaintances, by putting ourselves at the disposal of the Party and the ÁVH to help them fight the Imperialists more effectively.

'If you stop being so stubborn,' he concluded 'the Party will show you mercy. Already, tomorrow, you'll get better treatment. For instance, you will be given another cell, a blanket, decent food, meat. Think of it, man! meat! And you'll be spared a few things you probably don't enjoy too much. If not,' he shrugged his shoulders, 'you will have only yourself to blame. You will pay dearly. The choice is yours. I hope you understood me?'

My eyes were running in the blinding glare of the arc-light, my knees shook with exhaustion. I nodded to signify that I had indeed understood him. In franker, more unbiased language, reporting guesses or suspicions was equivalent to accusing each other on fictitious pretexts. And putting ourselves at the disposal of the ÁVH meant that we were to admit, without protest, any charge invented against us. Yet at that moment, all this appeared unimportant, uninteresting to me. Important, exclusively important, was to shut my eyes and stretch out on the wooden bunk of my cell, if only for a few moments.

These short rests always restored me a little, although when the interrogation took place at night, I could only rarely enjoy a brief nap during the day because the guards spared no effort to keep the inhabitants of the underground cells awake by banging the lids of the Judas-holes, and kicking the doors. In addition, I was suffering from constant, tearing pains in my chest and back, and particularly in the region of the kidneys, so that I had to muster all my strength to rise from the bunk. The skin on my swollen soles had cracked open in places; the rubber truncheons had burst the veins in my hands so that my palms had become inflated into dark purplish cushions and my fingers into sausages. For a week my kidneys discharged only blood, but my physical condition and the possible consequences of it caused me hardly any anxiety at all. My immediate concern was whether or not I would be allowed to sleep a little and whether they would take me up for questioning at the very time when they were distributing the morning soup or afternoon beans.

As I found out later, most of my fellow-prisoners in circumstances similar to mine were preoccupied, first and foremost, not with the problem of 'to be or not to be', but with the question to eat or not to eat, to be tortured or not to be tortured, and finally, to sleep or not to sleep. This was the state we were in when the young ÁVH officer indicated that basically it was up to the prisoner himself whether or not his lot improved. His concluding remarks offered a brittle golden bridge: the prisoner would yield not because he was afraid of torture, starvation and lack of sleep, but because he was eager to help his Party. The prisoner understood that though he himself was innocent, there were psychological reasons why, in a period of increased tension between East and West, the communists were suspicious of people who had studied and grown up in the West and who, during the war, had in any way co-operated with the Western allies.

In my eyes, Szönyi's statement, and even more Rajk's denial, justified the party's suspicions. However, this not only aggravated but also alleviated my situation in that it permitted a gleam of hope. If I remained firm, I might contribute to the separation of the innocent from those perhaps truly guilty among the communists of Western orientation who were, as a category, suspect; but if I admitted to trumped-up charges or, if simply by reporting guesses or suspicions, I furnished material for false accusations against others, I too would be responsible if suspicion and fact, truth and fiction, become inextricably mixed.

One night I was led up and down staircases, through corridors and a panelled passage-way into a part of the building that was wholly unfamiliar to me, though later I came to know it well. Turning sharp right on the landing we entered a spacious, oblong ante-room, passed a secretary bent over her typewriter, and the half-open door of the lavatory, and reached the chief's room. A fair-haired man in his mid-thirties, wearing the insignia of a Colonel, sat behind a desk. He told the guard to remove the chair facing the desk, then sent him from the room.

The Colonel's undistinguished but almost agreeable face was worn with fatigue, just like Károlyi's. His bloodshot eyes stared at me severely. For a few seconds I hoped that perhaps, at last, my case had reached the hands of a responsible person; that the ÁVH had compared the true facts with Szönyi's statement and that my interrogation would take a new turn.

'Who recruited you as an agent?' the Colonel asked suddenly.

After my now sterotyped reply, he barked at me:

'What was Wagner's message to Szönyi?'

When again I had nothing new to say, he did not wait for my answer to his third question: what letter had I brought Szönyi?—but produced a rubber truncheon from his desk drawer and issued an order:

'Hold out your hands! The other way round!'

The blows rained down on the backs of my hands, not on the palms. Then came the bastinado. While I was lying on the carpet, the Colonel bent over me:

'If you only knew how nice it looks when the truncheon sinks into your soles . . .' he whispered, then he gave my kidneys a few heavy blows with it.

He went back behind his desk, buttoned up his jacket and looked at me out of cold fish-like eyes.

'When did you meet Field? Noel Field?' he asked, enunciating every word precisely.

'I don't know him,' I replied.

'This Field is in our hands,' the Colonel declared loudly. 'That surprises you, doesn't it?'

I could only shrug my shoulders. I had never before heard the name of Field.

'But you will be even more surprised to learn,' my interrogator continued with a sarcastic smile, and his eyes lost their glassy stare, 'that we have also got hold of Field's archives. Amazing, isn't it? Even we were astonished at such carelessness on Field's part. Tell me, what was the text of the recruiting document?'

'I haven't the slightest idea.'

'Didn't you read it?'

'I never read such a document.'

'Not even before you signed it?'

'I never signed it . . .'

'And what would you say if I put this document, with your signature on it, on the table here? If I stuck it under your nose?'

I made no reply, but the Colonel insisted:

'Answer me! What would you say?'

'I should be surprised,' I answered in a low voice, although it would hardly have astounded me by now if I had been shown my own signature on a document leading straight to the scaffold. After all, if an unproved and unchecked statement was to be taken as evidence, why should not even the most obvious falsification be accepted as an authentic document?

The Colonel appeared to reflect; then, as if it had just occurred to him, he asked:

'How did you come back from America? Tell me in detail.'

I told him that it was because of visa and passport difficulties that I had remained in Argentina until 1946. In order to return home, I had to get permission, issued in Hungary, from the Allied Control Commission. To obtain this I corresponded with my friends in Budapest. I made no secret of it that I had written to László Rajk. However, this did not seem to interest the Colonel.

'By what route did you return home?'

'I went to France by ship, from there by train.'

'Through Switzerland, perhaps?'

'Yes, through Switzerland,' I replied. My interrogator was so pleased with my reply that his face brightened.

'Well,' he cried, 'then the whole thing is simple. Field was in Switzerland at that time. When you were passing through Switzerland, Field boarded the train and recruited you as his agent.'

I still don't know which nonplussed me more, the fact of the suggestion itself or its amazing naïveté. Both were frightening. More frightening, however, was the air of naturalness with which the Colonel suggested that I should confess to something he had just concocted with a complete disregard for even the shadow of truth.

It was hair-raising that he should be content with such a transparent fairy-tale. When I said that it appeared unimaginable to me that anyone should permit himself to be recruited into a foreign secret service by a complete stranger on a train, the Colonel shrugged his shoulders.

'If you don't like it, write something more convincing. I'll let you have paper and pencil. Write down who recruited you, when and how, and what was in the letter you brought Szönyi. Write down when and how frequently you met Szönyi since your return home; tell all you know about him and what you and he talked about. Write also about Field. We'll leave Rajk for another time. That should be enough for today.'

He made me sit down at a small table in his ante-room. He placed paper and pencil in front of me. A guard with a rifle kept watch. The secretary locked her drawer and left. I was often to sit hunched over that light-coloured, worn little table until daybreak. On the wall hung a large, idealized photograph of János Kádár. At the time, Kádár was still Minister of the Interior. A year and a half later he, too, became a political prisoner.

During the night there was little coming or going in the Colonel's ante-room. Once, however, I was interrupted by a young man clutching a large, brown envelope. He seemed in a great hurry. He looked around helplessly. The expressionless, exhausted, wooden features of the armed guard did not appear to inspire the newcomer's confidence, and in spite of my unshaven face, he must have thought I was one of his colleagues, for he turned to me, instead of the guard, and asked:

'Is Comrade László Farkas in his office?'

This is how I learned the name of the Colonel, though he continued to use the pseudonym Kovács when he telephoned in my presence.

No session passed without László Farkas making special mention of his proletarian background; this, together with his brief and insignificant participation in the anti-fascist resistance movement, he considered his greatest virtues and he liked to compare himself with my bourgeois family, education and interests. In fact, in his stiff, angular manner, he was always playing a part, except when he took out his truncheon. At such times a fierce, authentic flame blazed in his eyes and he was undoubtedly sincere when he hissed in my face:

'You just can't imagine how I hate you!'

On his desk, with typical petty-bourgeois taste, he kept a framed tinted photograph of his wife and small daughter. And on the wall of his office hung a portrait of the ascetic, bearded F. E. Dzerzinski, head of the Russian Cheka and afterwards of the GPU, whose murderous zeal even Lenin found exaggerated in 1923. At the peak of physical torture, Farkas's otherwise winsome smile, showing two rows of healthy teeth, distorted into a rigid, demonic grin. He would accompany every blow of the truncheon with remarks erupting from his infantile and vulgar sexual imagination; these, in the pauses between disconnected, obscene words, he would whisper in my ear or murmur to himself with enjoyment. After such scenes it took some time before he was able to shake himself back into his Dr. Jekyll state of mind, his everyday, eager, boyishly naïve, provincial garrison-officer personality, gazing out of dreamy, innocent eyes at the idyllic family group on his desk.

I must admit that I feared none of my interrogators as I feared Farkas. Once, after my release from prison, I ran into him at the entrance of the Kútvölgyi Sanatorium. I was sent there for a general check-up and met Farkas leading an elderly lady down the steps to a car bearing an official registration plate. The former ÁVH colonel had grown fat; his face was no longer pink but yellow. He reminded me now not of the boyish garrison-officer but rather of a prematurely aged, obese Russian general, fearful of being arrested. László Farkas was then organizing secretary of the Greater Budapest Party head-quarters and a member of the Central Committee – and even in 1956, just before the revolution, his name was often to be seen in the press and on posters announcing prominent speakers. When, for a moment, our glances met at the sanatorium entrance, his face did not break into the self-assured smile I had so often seen. It darkened.

On this first day of our acquaintance, too, the Colonel's face darkened as he read my draft.

'This is nothing,' he said, 'nothing at all!'

It was true the notes contained nothing new. I had summarized a few conversations I had had with Szönyi, and gone on to refute his statements first made at the foot of the T-shaped table, pointing out their utter absurdity. Of Noel Field I only said that I had never come across a person of that name. To be truthful, I did wonder for a moment whether it might not be more rational to fall in, partially at least, with the Colonel's suggestions. All the more so as the picture he had painted – Noel Field boarding the Arlberg Express and attempting to recruit a complete stranger for the American secret service, a Hungarian communist at that, returning home from the other side of the globe–might have furnished an amusing plot for a satirical film, but could never claim credence from normal human beings.

If I rejected the temptation it was by instinct rather than by careful consideration of the possible consequences. Since then, however, I have had the opportunity of comparing my experiences with those of others and today I feel certain that the idiotic suggestion concerning Field was a trap set not for the first time, the cleverness of which lay in its very guise of stupidity. As a matter of fact, some people, believing that even a People's Democratic court of law would feel ashamed at allowing such arrant nonsense to be taken seriously, laughed up their sleeve and accepted the role for which they were cast in the puppet-show. Then, in most cases, the silly story having served its subtle purpose, it was discarded without ever reaching the court; and, on the first admission, skilled artisans of the ÁVH constructed an inverted pyramid of fantastic charges, and though the bricks may have been baked from the soap-bubbles of imagination, their very weight sufficed to crush a slave of formal logic. Then, out of artistic pride rather than tactful consideration for the judge's sensitive conscience, the ÁVH investigators would drop the hotchpotch of nonsense and concoct a somewhat less incredible story to which the victim of logic–who had, by then, admitted to even graver crimes–would sign his name without protest.

As yet, my reflections had not strayed towards such possibilities when I ignored the Colonel's suggestion to write something more plausible. I don't know what he could have expected from me, nor do I know whether it was with feigned indignation or sincere fury that he flung my draft on the table, shouting:

'I'll show you how we deal with spies, traitors and police agents! From today you will stand, even in your cell! You will not lie down, either by day, or by night. No food. No water. No washing.'

He picked up the receiver then changed his mind and called the armed guard:

'Take the prisoner down.'

Then he followed us into the corridor.

'Don't let him get near the bannister,' he told the guard. 'Keep him close to the wall, he's already tried to finish himself off once.'

As the apprehensive guard took my arm and pushed me to the wall of the staircase, Farkas broke into hooting laughter. His guffaws echoed in my ears all the way down to the second floor.

3

The People's Educator

THAT night was followed by a period certain details of which it is vain to try to bring back from oblivion. This may be due in part to psychological factors, particularly the emotional economy of forgetfulness enabling a man to rid himself of tormenting memories and passions that could render him sleepless. Still, I may not be mistaken if I suppose that my physical condition was mainly to blame that my recollections become, here and there, hazy. But certain scenes and critical moments remain imprinted on my memory, both visually and acoustically, with the exactitude of a synchronized sound-film, and I can quote every word spoken at such moments. Therefore, I have no reason to fear that either forgetfulness or emotion will lead me astray.

As a result of the Colonel's order, I was once and for all freed from the anxiety whether or not I would get a few minutes sleep or whether I would miss the flour-soup in the morning and the beans in the afternoon. I was led to a remote cell, which nobody ever passed; the lid of the Judas-hole was left open and an armed guard stood almost uninterruptedly in front of the door. Later the door was left open, a bench was placed before it, and this is where the four members of a one guard-unit, uniformed men and civilians alike, set up quarters when on duty. Whether on instruction or simply for fun, they used me to relieve their boredom. They ordered me to stand motionless, then yelled at me or kicked the door, and on the pretext that I had moved, fell upon me and struck and kicked me all over. Other groups of guards left only the Judas-hole open, and one of the armed guards made me stand in front of the small opening so that he could spit in my face every time he went by.

After a few days, these spectacular doings must have gained fame in the cellar-township, for from time to time an expert audience assembled in front of my cell. Sometimes the guests grew tired of being merely spectators and took an active part in the proceedings. This is how, one day, I came to be visited by a broad-shouldered man in his mid-forties, whom the others called Tarján—in England, they would perhaps have called him Tarzan. His flattened nose and cauliflower ears betrayed that he had devoted his youth to the excitement of the ring rather than to the study of Virgil's Bucolics. Although he hardly came up to the level of my eyes, his physical strength was such that, to the delight of the grateful audience, he lifted me by the hair, swung me back and forth, and when my heels touched ground again, held me away from him at an angle of 45 degrees and bashed his fist several times into my face.

There were times when they made me stand facing the lamp, then again facing the whitewashed wall, sometimes with my back, sometimes with my side towards the door and the Judas-hole. On the third day I longed for water but had no longer any wish to eat.

On the fourth day, my eyes discerned a medley of colours on the white wall; then these pale and uncertain greens, yellows and pinks began gradually to form into pictures. One I particularly remember is the picture of a crowded terrace of a Champs Elysées café where, among mediaeval poets and contemporary painters, I saw Walt Whitman sitting at a small, round table, wearing a hat the size of a mill-stone and sipping lemonade through a long straw.

I realized even then that my eyes were conspiring with my imagination; that they were playing a game of benevolent cunning to distract my attention from the present. But when, through the open door of the cell, I stole a glance at the corridor wall and there, under a neo-classical bas-relief I read the signature of a sculptor friend of mine, it suddenly occurred to me that I might be having hallucinations. I wondered why they had arrested the sculptor and felt glad that he had a privileged position here, in the cellar, since he was permitted to work, if only with plaster. I observed with pleasure the slender female figures walking with a basket or a jug on their heads, though I wondered with some disapproval why my friend had reverted to his earlier, neo-classical style. It did not seem in the least strange that I should now notice his work, though the day before, the wall had still appeared smooth and empty.

It did not appear to me any less real than the bas-relief when I noticed that not only did the concrete floor of the cell show patches of dampness but that great puddles were forming on it; then my feet and the entire cubicle were flooded with a filthy liquid, the level of which rose gradually, until it reached my chest. There it stopped, began to recede, rose and receded again, and when, after much ebb and flow, once more there remained only tiny puddles on the floor, I observed that out of the concrete floor the water had washed century-old newspapers with old-fashioned typography and pictures of the nobility dressed in the fashion of our great-grandparents.

It is at this point that my recollections become hazy; I don't know when and how often I was taken up for questioning, I don't know how often the water in my cell rose to my chest then receded again, all I recall is that when the grey-haired interrogator opened the door and I made some remark that the old newspapers on the floor should be in a museum, and complained about the spitting guard, he pointed to the bunk and told me to lie down.

With this single exception, made memorable also by a full dixie of beans, I stood for nine days and nine nights without food and without water. These nine days must have been an event worth recording; perhaps they were set down in my file side by side with the date of my birth, since they were repeatedly referred to later by various investigators and, approximately a year and a half later, one of them promised that he would make me stand for another nine days, 'but this time on one foot'.

Since my arrest I had not been shaved, had not cut my nails, nor had I changed my underwear. Even before those nine days, the guards had frequently deprived the prisoners in the cellar of the few pleasant minutes of ablution; perhaps out of laziness rather than malice. But now Farkas's orders had put out of my reach even this modest possibility of cleaning myself. I touched with distaste the three week's growth on my face and looked with nausea at my swollen, deformed hands, my blackened nails. The extreme torment of filthiness was augmented by the fact that, as a result of the complete lack of food and water, my mouth was filled with a glue-like, sticky fur that impeded even my speech. Soon I was as unbearably disgusted with my own physical state as with the Colonel's frequent personality changes and obscene play of imagination when excited by cruelty.

Days and nights flowed into each other. Every time I heard the noises of the morning soup distribution I drew another line on the calendar scratched into the humid wall. At dawn, when I was being led back from an interrogation, I kept an exact record of the number of bastinados and palm-beatings, like a conscientious journalist, a chronicler, who may, sometime, somewhere, have to account for his experiences with professional honesty and reliable exactitude. Yet I wished nothing more ardently than never to see that cell-wall again, nor the guards nor the Colonel, and it would have seemed to me a saving joy if my heart had at last stopped beating. Of this I now saw some hope, for my ankles had swollen to the size of elephants' and my knees were like large melons, almost completely filling my trouser-legs. I concentrated all my energy upon interrupting and terminating my biological functions. Yet during those nine days, only once did I collapse and lose consciousness. But however hopeless I knew my situation to be, or perhaps just because of that hopelessness, I sometimes found the transports of rage, the primitiveness and cynicism of the Colonel, and even my own pedantic and utterly purposeless statistics amusing, and there were moments when I entertained myself, almost self-forgetful, with my time-killing games.

The permanent dialogue between the instinct of survival and the wish for liberating death was frequently interrupted by the knowledge that what the investigators and the Colonel were constantly repeating, namely that they were acting with the full approval of the Communist Party, was indeed true. They committed deeds of extreme cruelty in the name of a party that I had joined in my early youth because of a groping, radical humanitarianism. And yet, I felt that I had no more spiritual affinity with the guards in the cellar, the investigators, Vajda, Tarján, the Colonel, Károlyi, Ernö Szücs or Gábor Péter, than with an amoeba. I had never accepted the philosophy that considers the end justifies the means, and I therefore regarded it as all the more self-evident that the means applied by the ÁVH compromised any end whatsoever, for all time to come. As I myself would have prevented such procedure as theirs everywhere, at all times and against everyone, with passionate indignation, had I had the power to do so, I considered myself caught in a trap, betrayed, because, in however small a degree, and however indirectly, my communist past had been grist to Gábor Péter's mill. This realization only increased my wish that my breathing should at last stop.

For this reason, the death-wish remained dominant, but at the same time, the instinct of survival, and even more the immediate torment of thirst, compelled me to commit a shameful act. At certain times the guards conducted even me to the lavatory although on the third day of starvation and thirst my metabolism had almost completely ceased. I went only for the pleasure of moving about. But on one occasion I could no longer hold my animal desire in check; I pulled the chain and stuck my face into the bowl to get at least a few drops of water. In vain did my gaoler press the barrel of his revolver in the back of my neck, as long as the water was running, in vain did he kick me, pull me, and hit my head with the butt of his gun.

The physical agony and tormenting need of sleep, water and food, were supplemented by threats and promises. Farkas took particular pleasure in depicting in great detail various methods of torture inspired partly by his reading (for example, a translation of Octave Mirbeau's *Le Jardin des Supplices*), partly by his own imagination. He frequently described an instrument the invention of which he claimed for himself, the execution to the brilliant technicians of the ÁVH. This instrument, complete with straight-jacket, could, according to the Colonel, lift the eye-ball from its socket and introduce electrodes into the eye-hole thus causing inhuman suffering and insanity. While threatening me with the most varied tortures Farkas also declared several times – as his predecessors, particularly the grey-haired investigator had done before him – that not only myself but also my family would suffer the results of my stubbornness. My mother was already under arrest and my three-year-old son would be sent to a camp for children: neither I, nor his mother, nor our friends, would ever see him again.

'Do you think,' he asked me again and again, 'that we have to account to anyone for your family, your child or even your own life? Nobody and nothing obliges us to send a spy and a Horthy police agent for trial. If we don't get a statement, you will either rot away in this cellar or we shall take you out one night to some deserted place, make you dig your own grave, then shoot you in the back of the head. I can assure you that no-one will look for you. You will have disappeared, and that will be that.'

After this several times in the middle of the night my cell door was unlocked. Five or six grim-faced men would put me in irons, bundle me into a car and drive me out of town. Blinded by dark glasses I sat in the speeding car cramped between two security men and the car cornered sharply, first in the deserted streets and later on the winding road leading up the mountain; only the humming of the motor and the squeaking of brakes were audible, there was no sound of human voices or other traffic. At such times I thought not only of Farkas's threats, but remembered my religious childhood when I had prayed for an easy death. A bullet in the back of the head now seemed indeed easy. Usually however, I landed in the cellar of some secret villa because, especially in the mountains of Buda, the ÁVH had commandeered a large number of summer villas, like the one with the T-shaped table where I had spent my first days and had been confronted with Rajk. Gradually, I became inured to these nightly excursions and if, at first, I felt a shiver run down my spine, later I no longer even wondered whether I would return or not.

It could not have escaped the Colonel's attention that neither the prospect of having to dig my own grave before being shot, nor even the carrying out of this threat, was likely to appear more uncomfortable to me than my present situation. So, early one morning, after an exhausting all-night session, he put his little flat revolver on the desk in front of him and delivered the following speech:

'I am perfectly aware of your state of mind. You feel that everything has come to an end. That there is no way out. We know that you are a spy and were a Horthy police agent, and you know what is coming to you. We have sufficient proof. That reminds me, tomorrow I shall show you your recruiting document. But even so, if you decide to help me, if you make a statement, I promise that I will show you mercy. I shall leave you alone for five minutes with this gun. There will be one bullet in the magazine. Naturally, I shall remove the others.'

For a while he fumbled with the clip of his gun, then he looked at me.

'Don't you believe it? You don't believe me?' and he broke into loud laughter.

This scene was repeated several times in several variations, at dawn or at night. But once, as if no-one had ever said anything about a bullet in the back of the head, or out of mercy, leaving me alone with the revolver, the Colonel went to the wireless which stood next to the divan. He switched it on, and sank down on to the divan. It was late, most stations were broadcasting dance-music. The Colonel waited for the announcer to speak.

'Well, Mr. Scholar,' he asked, 'is that Spanish?'

'Italian.'

Farkas narrowed his eyes, examined the dial of the wireless closely, then turned the knob. The strains of a *jota* filled the room. We heard the Madrid announcer.

'It wouldn't be bad, would it,' the Colonel laughed, 'to sit on the terrace of a Madrid café, and perhaps stretch out on the sands on the Spanish coast. In the sun. And then bathe. Imagine! Bathe. For, no doubt, you know that you stink like a skunk?'

Then he grew serious, jumped up from the divan and began walking to and fro.

'If you make a statement involving yourself and others, we shall sentence you to a few years. You won't have it bad in prison, I'll take care of that personally. Because I need an able man to work for me, one I could send to Spain. You speak Spanish, you'd be most suitable. In a year, a year and a half, or even much earlier, I shall get you out of prison. Your family stays here, of course, and if you try to play any trick on me abroad, your boy . . .'

55

The Colonel stretched his arms forward and made a movement as if he were wringing a heavy, wet sheet. Then he looked at me.

'Well, would you like to work for me? Work in Spain?'

'I wouldn't know how,' I replied.

'Of course you would. You'd be excellent! I couldn't find anyone better. But you don't believe me. You don't want to work for me. Isn't it true that you don't believe me? Isn't it true that you don't believe I would release you from prison?'

I made no reply.

'All right,' said Farkas reaching for the rubber truncheon. 'You don't believe me and you don't want to work for me. In that case we shall get back to our good, old, reliable people's educator.'

Before swinging it, the Colonel tenderly caressed his favourite instrument which he had christened 'the people's educator', and for which he had a wide variety of loving nicknames. In those days, the people's educators of the Communist Party were the agitators who went to factories and other places of work, and even from house to house, trying to convince the doubters of the correctness of communist policies and of the uniquely redeeming quality of the ideals of Soviet socialism.

Colonel Farkas obviously regarded the ÁVH's blunter methods of persuasion as more expedient; though the fact that he made fun of a party institution like the people's educators with such impudent, cynical irony, might have led one to suppose that he believed in neither the communist dogma nor the world-transforming power of socialism, but had put himself at the service of the system merely as a mercenary. Though I think that such a supposition would not reflect the whole truth.

From the devout and emotional respect with which he recalled the events and personalities of the past when attempting to build a credible background for my alleged activities as a former police agent, I gained the impression that Farkas's cynicism was interwoven with some sort of bigoted and sentimental blind faith. It is questionable whether this flicker of religious enthusiasm was kept alive artificially, or whether, at times, he unconditionally and sincerely believed that he was a believer. I seemed to discover signs of the latter in numerous sudden softenings and indignations which reasons of duty could hardly have led him to put on, and in the tensely expectant, even anxious way in which he waited for my reply and watched for the effect, when by way of a detour he referred to some aspect of socialist ideology to show off his extensive reading.

But another duplicity was to have a more direct effect upon my fate than the ambivalence of Farkas's emotional make-up.

The Colonel urged me more and more openly to invent some story that would help to prove that I was a spy and a former Horthy police agent. He dreamed up, then discarded, different stories, suggested others, then discarded those as well. The variants excluded each other mutually, not merely psychologically, but also as far as place and time were concerned. This made it evident that his intention was to construct a false charge against me with complete disregard for the facts. At the same time, he had no doubts whatsoever as to my being a suspicious individual, not merely harmful but dangerous from the point of view of the Communist Party, a person to be eliminated; and that I had indeed committed acts that the political police were justified in punishing. At times, Farkas reminded one of a child given a puzzle to solve; he sought more and more savagely for the solution, knowing all the time that it must be a simple one, but, unable to find the right answer, he resorted to cheating rather than admit the shameful fact of his impotence.

He wanted results at any price; he must find compromising episodes in my life, give me a bad conscience over some insignificant detail, so that I would acknowledge the justification of their suspicion and thence draw the conclusion that I must, to appease my feeling of guilt, admit to a capital crime. Finally Farkas did indeed discover the damning evidence he wanted.

When he enquired into the circumstances of my various travels I readily recounted every detail, nor did I conceal the fact that when, in the spring of 1939, it was no longer easy for a Hungarian citizen to obtain an overseas visa, the military attaché of the Hungarian Legation in Paris, Colonel Karátson, one-time class-mate of a close relation of mine at the Military Academy, had helped me, at the request of my army-officer relatives, to obtain an entry permit for the Argentine.

Farkas made me relate with hair-splitting accuracy my conversations with Colonel Karátson. Although my talks with the military attaché turned almost exclusively on our common interest, film-making, Farkas made me repeat again and again what Karátson had said, what I had said, how I came to introduce the attaché to the chairman of the French amateur film club; when and how we attended exclusive meetings when, at the film-club, they screened the prize-winning avant-garde films of the year. I also recounted repeatedly and in minute detail my exclusively formal visit to the Argentinian military attaché for, naturally, Karátson introduced me to his Argentinian colleague, and innumerable times I described my brief talk with the Argentinian consul to whom, in turn, I was introduced by the Argentinian military attaché.

The very fact—Farkas concluded—that I had come into contact, socially, with people of that sort, put me in a doubtful light. He, for instance, could never have entered such suspicious and compromising circles. It put me in an equally bad light, and this even I had to admit, that since 1933 I had had no direct organizational contact with the Communist Party either in Hungary or in France; all I did was to contribute a few articles to leftist publications and deliver a few lectures in fellow-traveller clubs. It was characteristic, Farkas added, that even for these articles and lectures, I selected art subjects and not political or sociological ones. Even so, according to his information, my lectures had aroused general uproar and indignation. I ought to see the condemning depositions made against me by communists who had returned from France and Argentina; my hair would stand on end if I knew what a vile and despicable Trotskyite they took me for.

It must be clear even to me, Farkas continued, that no man in his right mind would believe that a military attaché would do someone a favour merely out of friendship. Military attachés are professional spies, therefore, there could be no shadow of doubt that Karátson would help me only if I did espionage work for him in exchange. At the same time, a military attaché must protect his reputation. He would not openly ask a complete stranger for information, in case by doing so, he should be led into a trap. It was quite obvious that the attaché knew I was an old and experienced agent. All he did was take me over from Peter Hain, the head of the detective branch of the Hungarian political police. For as far back as 1932, when as a young communist, I was arrested, Peter Hain had recruited me into the service of the Horthy régime as an *agent provocateur*. Karátson helped me to obtain an Argentinian visa, partly in reward for my services, partly to spy for him in South America, but by no means selflessly, or without an ulterior motive.

How could I have been Peter Hain's agent, I asked, if, as the Colonel himself had disapprovingly remarked, 'I maintained no close contact with the communists?' What could I have told Hain about them? What information could I obtain for Karátson in the class-rooms of the Sorbonne?

'Just at present,' the Colonel interrupted me, 'we are not discussing your espionage activities but the circumstances under which you were recruited as an agent.'

He had shaped, then re-shaped, changed and pieced together the story of my recruitment for several days now. He referred no longer to Szönyi's statement, he asked no questions concerning Wagner, Field, or Wagner's fictitious message to Szönyi. He was content to prove that I was a man of doubtful antecedents, that they were justified in suspecting me, and that it should be entirely a matter of indifference to me how the deposition expressing the party's suspicion of me was formulated, for even if that suspicion remained no more than suspicion, I should never again be released. I was in the power of the ÁVH, they could do with me as they pleased, they could starve me to death in the damp cellar, and if they finished me off more quickly I should owe them a debt of gratitude.

After I had been standing for seven times twenty-four hours, they no longer led, but half dragged, half carried me to Farkas's room. If, after the now ritual bastinado I was unable to rise, the Colonel pushed a chair towards me with his foot. To make me understand how much he loathed me he did not touch it with his hands. I would then get hold of the leg of the chair, pull myself up to the seat then grasp the back of the chair and straighten up relying solely on the strength of my arms. Two of the lower ribs in my chest had completely caved in and now rendered my stomach muscles almost useless.

'Are you shamming? What's the matter with you?' Farkas asked, pretending surprise.

'I must have some broken ribs,' I replied.

'If you had, you wouldn't be able to stand,' he declared with the superior assurance of the expert.

He was wrong. A good five years later, side by side with other injuries the X-ray pictures showed the ungainly scars of two broken ribs in my chest, and three in my back. However, during my interrogations it never even occurred to me to bother about such petty details. What did I care who was right, when, on the eighth and ninth day of constant standing Farkas was promising me pleasures undreamed of. As soon as he had finished his statement dealing with Colonel Karátson, he said, I would get a jug of hot cocoa and a piece of plain cake.

And on the night of the ninth day he summoned his secretary, sending his car to fetch her. The frighteningly ugly, bespectacled girl took her place beside the Colonel's desk. She stared grimly at the keys of her typewriter as if she feared the fate of Lot's wife, should her eye accidentally fall on me. In marked contrast, the Colonel giggled happily, allowed himself childish jokes, and sucked lumps of sugar while dictating his notes which–if I remember rightly–dealt with my family background, university years and the events of the student movement, particularly László Rajk and my conversations with him.

I was lying on the floor, dozing, and came to with a start only when Farkas yelled at me, called my name, or reminded me of the cocoa and cake. Though I looked up at such times, I had no hope whatever of touching that cocoa or that cake. Not only because I had little faith in the Colonel's promises, but also because in my half-stupor it seemed to me utterly inconceivable that such pleasures should ever again exist for me in reality, instead of in the realm of fantasy.

I was no longer able to follow Farkas's dictation or to concentrate my attention for more than a few seconds. Only the memory of my earlier reflections still turned round and round in my mind. Slowly, with great effort, I attempted to piece them together. The methods applied in the past three weeks had the purpose of reducing me, the suspect, both physically and mentally, to such an animal condition that my momentary needs would deprive me of human dignity and render me blind; they were aimed at distorting my judgment of values, at falsifying my standards when differentiating between rational and irrational, so that an hour's sleep seemed a greater treasure than life itself, and where, in exchange for a little peace or a jug of cocoa, or to escape from the terror of physical pain, I would confess even to a charge involving the noose. But by now, all things had become a matter of indifference to me. As long as I could close my eyes, lying there on the floor, I gladly forgot even the cocoa. I was awakened by Farkas. He called my name several times in succession:

'You are not paying attention,' he said without anger, then screwed up his eyes ironically, 'though we shan't be long now. We have reached Péter Hain. Come, tell me how he recruited you? Did he give you a cover-name?'

Though I made no reply Farkas continued to dictate; then like a railway guard bawling the name of the station, he called to me again:

'What did that Karátson look like? Describe him again. Get up!'

I crawled to the chair, got hold of its leg and pulled myself to my feet in the usual way.

'We are having a beautiful dawn, or rather morning,' Farkas smiled almost benevolently and rubbed his eyes, bloodshot from lack of sleep. 'You may look out.'

Indeed, the Colonel's balcony was bathed in brilliant sunshine and the sun shone on the floor of the room, too. Farkas came to my side.

'You may look out,' he encouraged me, 'certainly you are not able to jump out,' he added; nonetheless, he followed me as I stumbled towards the light.

The whole length of Andrássy Street was sparkling in the sunshine and red geraniums were sunning themselves on the window-sills and on the balcony.

'Another hour, and you'll have your cocoa and cake. I am a man of my word,' Farkas assured me, then went back to his desk to continue dictating to the grim girl.

I don't know how many more pages he dictated. But though I never saw the promised cocoa I cannot say that the Colonel was not a man of his word, that he deliberately deceived me, because, for my part, I never signed the final text of the legend concerning Péter Hain and Colonel Karátson. But on this brilliant morning, the struggle was not yet over; it was merely interrupted by the sudden ringing of the telephone.

Farkas lifted the receiver, and answered with military brusqueness; he was almost standing to attention. Then he quickly arranged his papers and locked them up. He whispered something to his secretary, buttoned and smoothed down his tunic and gave me a signal:

'Let's go!'

As I was stumbling down the stairs he came to my side, grasped my arm and spoke in a low voice:

'Don't try to play it smart with the Lieutenant-General! If you do, you'll pay for it.'

When we turned from the corridor into the ornate mirrored lobby leading to Gábor Péter's ante-room, the Colonel stopped for a second. I stopped, too. And then, from the long mirror on my right, I saw a stranger looking back at me from hollow eyes in an unkempt, bearded face. He wore my grey suit and it was many sizes too large for him; when I touched the button of my jacket, he copied the action. It was some time before I could convince myself that I was facing my own image in the mirror.

Behind the padded door, Gábor Péter sat at a desk facing the entrance; next to him and behind him, a few leading ÁVH officers. I recall Ernö Szücs's face, Vladimir Farkas's and Dr. Bálint's, but others may have been present also. László Farkas placed himself some distance away from me, near the left-hand window opening on Andrássy Street. To the right of me stood a round table. On it were some twenty-five telephones of various shapes and sizes, which, for a second, suggested that the grim men assembled here were engaged in arranging some modest technical exhibition.

I can scarcely remember what Gábor Péter asked me, for, as soon as he offered me a chair and I could sit down, I suddenly felt as if curtains of spider-web thinness were being let down before my eyes, one behind the other in quick succession, and from second to second it became more difficult to penetrate them. Soon, I caught myself falling and had to hold fast to the seat of the chair. Still, I went on answering the questions put to me, until Gábor Péter lost patience:

'Nonsense,' he cried angrily at one of my answers, then added after closer observation:

'What's the matter with you?'

When I remained silent, he insisted on knowing what had happened. I told him that I was tired, exhausted, because I had been standing for nine full days and nights, and, with the exception of one break, without food or water.

'On whose orders?' Ernö Szücs's and Gábor Péter's voices rose in wrath simultaneously.

All eyes turned towards László Farkas, then the Lieutenant-General looked at me and pointed to the door:

'Leave the room,' he said.

I stumbled out into the ante-room, then, without asking for permission, threw myself into the same deep purple armchair in which, on that first day, I had waited while the security man telephoned from Gábor Péter's room. Within seconds I fell into a deep sleep.

I was awakened by a diminutive little man. At the time he fulfilled the functions of an orderly and valet to the Lieutenant-General. Later, in reward for his services, he was appointed director of the Gyüjtö or Concentration Prison housing political prisoners. It was there I learned that he was called Antal Bánkuti, and my cellmate, a social-democrat steel-worker from Diósgyör, told me that during the war years Bánkuti had been an employee at the Diósgyör steel-works, a sort of record-keeper. At that time he boasted of his clerical job just as he did later of his past as a manual worker. Bánkuti led me back to his chief's room. I sat down. Dr. Bálint addressed me:

'What kind of drug are you addicted to?'

I did not understand the question and when Bálint insisted on knowing whether I had not been taking some drug, or some medicine containing a drug, I thought this interrogation was also part of the cat and mouse game. Gábor Péter did not seem particularly interested in this interlude, for as soon as Bálint paused, he motioned to him to be silent and turned to me:

'Look here. You are going to sleep now and you will also get some food.'

'I should like to shave,' I said.

'You can't, but someone will shave you.'

'And take a bath . . .'

'You can take a bath and you'll get clean underwear.'

Bánkuti took me under my armpits again and led me to a bathroom where I could take a hot shower and cut my nails. He brought me a clean shirt and pants. Then they took me to a small room where I was shaved and afterwards they put me to bed on an iron cot with a sheet and blankets, in an office or inspection room, with an armed guard to watch me.

At regular intervals, they woke me. I was given tea and biscuits, coffee with lots of milk and rolls, and later mashed foods. It was evident that the diet had been prescribed by a physician. Did Gábor Péter remember, and in a sudden burst of enthusiasm take seriously what Mátyás Rákosi, the First Secretary of the Hungarian Communist Party so often proclaimed, namely that 'in the people's democracy man is the greatest asset'? Hardly. And though Colonel László Farkas may indeed have been taken to task by his chief, it was presumably not for his application of the classical ÁVH methods, but because the Colonel's ideas on people's education had endangered a life still of value to the ÁVH. Not, of course, in the general meaning of Rákosi's slogan but because it seemed suitable material to fit into a plan that was beginning to take shape.

On the sunny morning when the Colonel accompanied me to the Lieutenant-General's room, even the newspaper-reading public may have guessed that something was afoot, for the official organ of the Hungarian Communist Party, the *Szabad Nép*, published the following brief but conspicuous communiqué under the heading: 'Resolution of the Hungarian Workers' Party's Central Committee and Central Control Commission', and sub-heading: 'Unmasking of a Trotskyite espionage ring':

The Central Committee has expelled László Rajk and Tibor

Szönyi, as spies of foreign imperialist powers and Trotskyite agents from the ranks of the Hungarian Workers' Party.

The prisoners of the ÁVH were not informed of this sensation; no newspaper ever reached their hands. And if, by any chance, I had not been sleeping in a bed, on a sheet on that day, but had still been standing in the cellar, I should have done nothing other than engrave on my calendar the date: June 16, 1949; and in my statistics, under the heading *soling*, I should have marked the thirty-sixth (neglecting to add that one *soling* consisted of 15–25 blows of the truncheon, though if performed by the Colonel only 15–18) and under the heading *palm-beatings*, I should have reminded myself with five thick lines that I had, with luck, weathered half a thousand.

For over two days and two nights, I slept in a stupefied torpor, yet in an agony of restlessness. I opened my eyes only when they woke me to give me food. On the third day, one of the guards spoke a few words to me; I replied, and then immediately, as if there were no more important task imaginable than keeping a diary and I had to make good a criminal omission, I asked what date it was. The armed guard proved kind and allowed me to share the secret that it was the 18th of June. In all probability the second communiqué which both party-members and non-party members were to read on the 19th of June on the third page of *Szabad Nép* was already written:

> The press-department of the Ministry of the Interior announces: For espionage carried out on behalf of foreign powers, the State Security Organization has arrested László Rajk, Dr. Tibor Szönyi, Pál Justus and 17 accomplices. There is no industrial worker or peasant among those arrested.

The concluding sentence, which, by the way, did not coincide with the truth, 'there is no industrial worker or peasant among those arrested,' created panic, overt and covert, among white collar workers and intellectuals.

In the following weeks, *Szabad Nép* and other newspapers carried reports of hundreds of spontaneous demonstrations and mass-rallies, of an avalanche of letters and telegrams received, in which citizens, factories and organizations of the country expressed their 'savage hatred for the Trotskyite traitors' and begged the Party and the authorities to 'strike down with ruthless energy this vile gang of spies and imperialist agents'. The Party's central organ opened a permanent column for protests and attracted attention to the more important ones by giving them banner headlines: 'There is no room for mercy for the traitor Rajk and his gang. We request the Political Committee and Comrade Rákosi to leave not even the seed of treason in our Party', (*Szabad Nép*, 24th June, 1949). At their meeting, Greater Budapest Party 'condemned the traitors with ardent hatred, and expressed their unlimited confidence in and devoted loyalty to the Central Committee and Comrade Rákosi', then, in a draft resolution, congratulated Rákosi who had set an example in militant communist vigilance', (*Szabad Nép*, 26th June, 1949). At the same time, however: 'The filth of the country, the reactionaries of all walks of life still living among us, have suddenly begun to speak of Rajk and his gang with pity', (*Szabad Nép*, 24th June, 1949). Not so the members of the Women's Federation: 'The working women loathe the gang of spies now unmasked because it is an enemy of the powerful socialist Soviet Union and the Party, the pledges of our peaceful, free future.' Therefore, the Women's Federation besought the party and the authorities 'to deal the imperialist agents a heavy blow', (*Szabad Nép*, 26th June, 1949).

While the interrogations were in full swing at the ÁVH, in the secret villas, and in the cellars of 60, Andrássy Street – where I, too, was taken back on the morning of 18th June – while tormented, lonely, starving men and women sat gazing at the electric bulbs and the dripping walls, the Monday journal of the Communist Party declared: 'The Judas Tito and the executioner Rankovich have introduced a fascist reign of terror in Yugoslavia', (*Független Magyarország*, 20th June, 1949), and *Szabad Nép* came out with the sensational headline: 'Witch-hunt in America – eleven communists in the dock', (*Szabad Nép*, 26th June, 1949). While the ÁVH were arresting approximately two hundred persons, reports appeared in the Hungarian Party press: 'The UDB – Tito's Gestapo – carried off its victims like a beast of prey. In Montenegro, in the environment of Andrijevica, sixty persons disappeared in a single day.' Then came heart-rending descriptions of the Yugoslav prisons where only rarely was permission given for 'families to bring in food and clean underwear', (*Szabad Nép*, 29th June, 1949). In the meantime, party-members and non-members alike were given ideological instruction. 'At an inspiring ceremony marking the commissioning of new officers of proletarian background', the Muscovite Mihály Farkas, Minister of Defence, following in the ideological footsteps of the pioneer theoretician József Révai thus clarified the concept of patriotism on behalf of these worker and peasant lads:

Only he who deeply loves the Soviet Union, the great protector of the world's peoples, the powerful and invincible vanguard of progress and peace, is a good Hungarian patriot. Only he is a good Hungarian patriot who reveres and loves our great teacher, Generalissimus Stalin, who successfully leads the struggle of the peoples for a lasting peace and the triumph of freedom in the entire world. (*Független Magyarország*, 18th July, 1949)

The reader was informed also that, in unhappy contrast to the Soviet Union fighting for the triumph of freedom, there were also police states. 'The USA is the greatest police state,' proclaimed a fat headline in the party organ, and this is how it summed up its proofs: '. . . the FBI drives thousands of innocent persons to suicide, terrorizes the entire country and in fact legalizes every successful gangster-trick, from threats to anonymous denunciation', (*Szabad Nép*, 24th July, 1949).

While the inhabitants of Budapest and the people of the Hungarian countryside were supplied with such exact information concerning an overseas country, they could not even guess what was happening to those of their relatives arrested by the ÁVH. Not only was it impossible to take them, even once in a while, such food or clothing as was accepted by the jailers of 'Tito's Gestapo'; they did not know whether those who had disappeared were held prisoner in Hungary or in the Soviet Union, or even if they were still alive. At 60 Andrássy Street, all information was refused.

4

'Imperialist Agent. Establish This!'

IT seems to me that communist state-management could best be depicted not as a static pyramid but rather as an area of concentric magnetic rings in which centrifugal and centripetal forces fluctuate simultaneously. This scheme of things is ideal when a single person—a dictator—stands at the centre. Where the hub of the concentric fields is no longer a fixed point but a small inner circle, each constituent element of this inner circle will generate separate concentric fields around itself which will frequently cut across each other. This illustrates the conflicts, alliances and struggles between the various factions which, in the outer circles, usually manifest themselves merely in the form of competition for authority.

In 1949, at least as far as appearances were concerned, the paradigm could be regarded as ideal because at its centre stood Stalin who, according to Mihály Farkas, was 'successfully' leading not only the Soviet Union and her satellites, but 'the struggle of all peoples for a lasting peace, the triumph of freedom throughout the world'. Which, being interpreted, means that Stalin was trying to extend the power-line network of the magnetic fields generated around himself, to the entire world. Because the world's population is the outer circle. According to communist theory, Stalin was the only begotten leader of the hundreds of millions; forming the closer circle is the working-class, or, to be more exact, the industrial workers. And the élite of the working class, to use Lenin's now liturgical formulation, is the Communist Party.

The printed pamphlets, the devout proclamations, invariably coupled the concept of the Communist Party with Stalin; and in Hungary they tagged Rákosi's name on to Stalin's. It was never mentioned that the ÁVH considered itself to be the élite of the Communist Party just as, according to the dogma, the party was the *avant-garde* of the working class. Yet, in 1948 it had already become clear in Hungary that, as far at least as the seizure of power was concerned, it was not the one million strong Communist Party, of heterogeneous composition, that was heir of the former underground élite. It transpired that the real successor of the secret, conspiratorial

67

party, demanding blind discipline, was none other than the equally secret, conspiratorial political police who demanded the same kind of blind discipline. The ÁVO, and its successor, the ÁVH.

From 1945 to 1948, following Rákosi's infamous 'salami-tactics', the Communist Party strove to dismember all other political parties and fill key positions in the state organization with its own men. After 1948, the same fate overtook the group of communist leaders not trained in Moscow. For by then, numerous bridge-heads of the state organization, seized by the communists from the bourgeois and other parties, had gradually been taken over by the political police. This was done in two ways: by transferring many members of the ÁVH to posts in the state administration; and by coercing into its service as informers many communists, though preferably members of other parties – formally still in existence in 1948 – and non-party members working in the various ministries.

The expansion of the political police was not even concealed. For example, several of us were transferred from the Ministry of Foreign Affairs immediately after Tamás Mátrai and other secret police had inundated the various sections of the Foreign Ministry and the Hungarian Embassies abroad. By the time I was appointed to the Ministry of Agriculture, the ÁVH reorganization there was more or less complete. The head of the personnel-department was a former ÁVH captain, who had been a shop-salesman, the transport section was directed by a former ÁVH captain, the control section by a former ÁVH first-lieutenant and the administration department by a former ÁVH major who had, in the past, been doing a shady business in cameras in Budapest's flea-market, the infamous Teleki-Square. These ÁVH officers, together with many of their colleagues of lower rank, had been transferred to the Ministry of Agriculture more or less simultaneously. Not one of them knew anything about agrarian problems; on the contrary, all were city dwellers who had never so much as smelled a village. They qualified for the high positions they held in the Ministry of Agriculture by having had a hand in staging the show-trial of the old and expert Ministry officials.

These former ÁVH officers continued to be as ignorant in matters of agriculture as they had been before their promotion, but they built up a network of spies in various sections of the Ministry, co-operated with other ÁVH agents who had been smuggled in earlier and less conspicuously, and recruited new agents – as for instance one of my secretaries – and, like Mátrai in the Foreign Ministry, maintained direct contact with the ÁVH headquarters. They always turned to the ÁVH for advice and always carried out the instructions of their headquarters, to the infinite despair of the party and non-party experts in the Ministry.

It was by these and similar methods that the ÁVH won ground in the state organizations and public offices. Naturally, this could not have been done without the knowledge of Moscow and the Muscovite party leaders. It was, in fact, carried out under direct orders from Moscow, on the basis of plans long elaborated. For the Hungarian secret police was set up in 1944 by MVD officers who arrived from Moscow with the Soviet armies and remained under their control. While the war against Hitler was still being waged on two fronts, direct Russian control could be established relatively discreetly, owing to the conspiratorial character of the secret police, and it was allowed to develop even while the democratic parties still held some power in Hungary. Thus, by 1949, the Russian MVD and the Hungarian communists who had returned from Moscow, most of whom were closely linked with the MVD, had made the ÁVH into a party within the party. It was not the one-million-strong Hungarian Communist Party, nor its successor, the Hungarian Workers' Party that made possible the Russian seizure of power in Hungary, but the party within the party: the political police and its trusted agents. For in Hungary the secret police was not merely an accessory of the Russian seizure of power, but an indispensable prerequisite, a *sine qua non*.

The last phase of the ÁVH seizure of power took place in 1948-9, when it occupied the key positions of the state administration in order to provide Moscow with a direct *chain of command* from the inner circle to the outer, and now no deceptive façade was necessary any longer. We must agree with Rákosi: this was, indeed, the 'year of change' in Hungary.

In the interests of the smooth functioning of the controlling structure, it became necessary for all persons suspected of, or capable of, resistance to be removed as a preventive measure. By 1949, Rákosi had succeeded in excluding the representatives of the democratic parties from the state administration. Those who remained no longer represented their parties but only themselves, and most of them had given in to the Muscovite leaders. Thus, thanks to their position in the state administration, it was, in the first place, the old Hungarian communists like Rajk and his friends, never recruited by the MVD, who were liable to resist, men who had lived in the West, who had learned the democratic rules of the game, and believed that their posts not only allowed them, but obliged them to think for themselves and even to show initiative and form decisions according to their notions of justice and fairness.

In utter contrast to these men, the young ÁVH officers were trained by their superiors for devotion, blind discipline, and were at the same time filled with a consciousness of mission and professional pride. In 1949, these young and usually newly-fledged communist ÁVH officers not merely regarded themselves as a select body, but their arrogance vied with the haughtiness of the mediaeval Hungarian bannerets. Their self-confidence was further inflated by the fact that they could fill their pockets with various allowances, bonuses and benefits, adding up to many times the earnings of a Hungarian office-worker or skilled industrial worker. Colonel Gyula Décsi, a member of Gábor Péter's inner circle, once told an official of the Ministry of Foreign Affairs that, on a realistic basis of comparison, the rank of a young ÁVH lieutenant equalled that of a legation secretary, that of a first lieutenant the rank of a legation counsellor, that of a captain the rank of an Ambassador; that a post in the Foreign Ministerial Service could equal the rank of an ÁVH major was not conceivable.

This financially pampered organization indoctrinated with a consciousness of mission, regarded the steering of the communist state as its natural privilege and was not only theoretically an élite, like the Hungarian Workers' Party, but in reality an élite within an élite, because, by 1949, its hand undoubtedly controlled the most vital switchboards of the state machinery. Therefore, for the members of the ÁVH, 'Party' was not merely an abstract idea, a theoretical and practical framework of ideas, as it was for the faithful Party-members; it was also a collective term, embracing the concrete notions 'our power', 'our prosperity,' 'our career,' which was raised by some of the ÁVH officers to the rank of some kind of mystical religious ideal.

After my release, in the summer of 1956, when Stalin had been dead for over three years, and Gábor Péter, Károlyi and Décsi were in prison, when Beria had already been executed and Rákosi sacked, and it seemed as though the unchangeable was, after all, changeable, several ÁVH officers indulged in self-justifying, even unsolicited, declarations. This is how I came to know, among others things, what took place inside the political police organization before the arrest of László Rajk and his fellow-accused.

In the records of the ÁVH, the Rajk affair differed from the previous show-trials staged in Hungary by involving members of the Hungarian Communist Party, and especially veteran communists.

Until then, the secret police had arrested and brought to trial almost exclusively persons like Cardinal Mindszenty who had often openly opposed the régime. In the Rajk affair only communists were arrested and leading communists at that, of whom, for people in their right minds, it was difficult to believe that they could be enemies of the system. Nor could the head of the ÁVH find anything in their files, apart from fictitious spy-reports and transparent hints and guesses, often from dubious sources.

Therefore, on the eve of the arrests – as I was told in 1956 by an ÁVH officer who was present – Gábor Péter called together his conspiratorial circle, stiffened with some of his most reliable men. He appealed to the party-loyalty of those assembled, to their unlimited trust in the party leaders, in Stalin and his Hungarian disciples. He stressed that the persons invited to this confidential conference, the élite of the élite within the élite, had been greatly honoured because the Party had selected them to accomplish an unusual task. The Soviet and Hungarian party leaders – Gábor Péter explained – had uncovered within the Hungarian Workers' Party an anti-party group, a monstrous conspiracy which, had its plans succeeded, would have endangered the very existence of the party. However, thanks to the communist vigilance of the leaders, the tables could still be turned and the communists could deal the imperialists, and their hireling, Tito, a terrible blow. The Russian and Hungarian comrades possessed confidential information as to the persons involved in the conspiracy; they knew who the agents of the foreign powers were. The unravelling of the details would be the task of the ÁVH. Gábor Péter expressed his hope that they would be worthy of the trust that had been placed in them.

Apart from the assurance that the party was infallible, Gábor Péter could put no fact, no proof, at the disposal of his men. Still, it was inconceivable for any ÁVH officer to reply in the negative to the question: 'Don't you believe the Party?' For, on the one hand, the existence of the ÁVH, the moral justification for any deed they committed, rested on their faith in the party; on the other hand, every communist secret police officer is fully aware that he is risking his life if he replies: 'No, I don't believe the Party', or even if he expresses the slightest doubt concerning the reliability of the information possessed by the Party. He may lay himself open to suspicion of protecting the so-called anti-Party group, or even of being a member of that group.

Péter stressed emphatically that the unmasking of the conspirators was of vital interest to the Party. To the members of the élite, there was nothing equivocal about that speech. It was clear to them that if they refused the honourable task, or attempted, under however cunning a pretext, to evade putting their services at the disposal of present party-interests, they would, in fact, be refusing to protect their own power and financial privileges, and their colleagues would regard them as renegades and deal with them as one deals with a front-line soldier who tries to desert to the enemy.

But it did happen–although I know of only one or two isolated cases–that certain ÁVH officers attempted to withdraw from the task thrust upon them, and there was even one case of suicide; but these incidents could scarcely be regarded as typical. Yet, each ÁVH officer must have been rather surprised when he opened the file of the suspect entrusted to his care. Except for a few scraps of gossip concerning the love-life of the arrested person, all he found was a little slip of paper, bearing a brief instruction in the hand of Mihály Farkas, Muscovite Minister of Defence:

X. Y. Imperialist agent. Establish this! Farkas.

Which meant that the innermost circle, in close collaboration with Moscow, had already decided on its verdict. The business of the secret police was to construct an indictment that matched the verdict: *X. Y. is an Imperialist agent. Establish this.* They had to 'realize' the allegation on that slip of paper in the same way as centuries ago a King's messenger used to unroll a sealed document and read a coherent text to the illiterate peasants. To establish, or, as they liked to call it, to 'realize' is to execute the verdict as the builder executes the plans of the architect, in which not even the architect or the engineer prescribes how the mason should place one brick upon the other.

Not every ÁVH officer was privileged to see Mihály Farkas's written order. After the conference and the general pep-talk, once their tasks were allotted, Szücs or Gábor Péter would usually give the group-leaders individually a verbal account of the 'confidential information of the Soviet and Hungarian comrades', such as, for example, that the accused entrusted to the care of this or that group-leader had been a police spy under Horthy and had later become the agent of this or that foreign power. Péter and Szücs might sometimes inform the officer, but at other times they only hinted, with what other persons the accused should be connected, in what way or ways he could be compromised or made to compromise others. They might even add that the written documents concerning the recruitment of the accused as a spy were preserved in the Moscow archives and would, when the time came, be put at the disposal of the ÁVH.

The innermost ÁVH circle–Gábor Péter, Szücs, Károlyi, Décsi and their fellows thought it important that the outer ÁVH circles–the investigators for instance who tortured me at the villa of the T-shaped table, and in the cellar of 60, Andrássy Street–should really believe that they were dealing with genuine spies. They were to believe this at least in *the first phase of the realization*. By various internal farces and utterly superfluous rules of a disciplinary nature, intended to create spectacular effects, they sought to carry out this aim. They even furthered it by dramatic manoeuvres such as the one carried out at my flat, after my arrest.

It seems that the inner ÁVH circle did indeed succeed in awakening in the investigators a sense of real danger and instil into them the belief that they were investigating a genuine, important espionage-affair. This explains why, at the villa of the T-shaped table, after the theatrical confrontation with Szönyi, intended partly to convince the security men, they attacked me with such apparently authentic fury, when trying to compel me, sworn enemy of 'our power', 'our prosperity', 'our career', to account for Wagner and Wagner's message to Szönyi.

But the Hungarian ÁVH leaders staging the drama, although a light-year away from the magnetic power-fields of the MVD inner circles, not to mention their centre, Stalin, did not imagine for a single moment that there was even a delicate link tying the verdict to reality and the charges of espionage and conspiracy were intended for the benefit of the outer ring of the ÁVH and the public. They were fully aware from the outset that the casual relation between the charges and the verdict was the exact opposite of bourgeois custom: the accusation was the consequence of the verdict, and not the verdict the outcome of proven charges.

The concentric ÁVH circles around the inner command either guessed or did not guess this. But, at least at first, the very outer circle of the ÁVH formed by the armed and uniformed men, appeared utterly unsuspecting. These men were often transferred from the regular army first to the frontier-guards of the ÁVH and eventually, to headquarters. Here they were tested and trained, and if they seemed suitable, were promoted to investigators, thus obtaining unlimited opportunities to make a career. This centripetal movement was made permanent by the constant increase of the ÁVH effective.

Though Colonel Farkas did not belong to the inner command, he came within one of the inner circles. He hovered on the periphery of the command and hoped that his ruthlessness and his results would one day promote his entry to the sacrosanct inner circle. When he took over my interrogation personally, Farkas, if I am not mistaken, did not as yet perform his duties with the disdainful cynicism of the top ÁVH men. He at first acted with conviction. During the months in which I frequently saw him he was advancing rapidly from a state of waning faith towards complete cynicism.

Later, the outer circles of the ÁVH also followed him along this road. I am relying not merely on my own experience; dozens of my fellow prisoners told to me how during their preliminary detention they witnessed the transformation of their ÁVH officers; how these exalted novices turned from enthusiastic believers into disillusioned, blasé and unfeeling craftsmen, manufacturing false charges. This process was unavoidable, because the more people were arrested, the more ÁVH investigators had to be employed, so the broader became the circle aware of what was happening behind the scenes until even the scene-shifters of the most limited mental capacity could no longer ignore it. But by the time the formerly convinced and enthusiastic ÁVH investigator fully woke up to reality, he had become an accomplice–and therefore a prisoner–of the inner circle to such an extent that it would have been extremely dangerous to try and sever his ties unilaterally. This is why the ÁVH bosses did not mind the gradual enlightenment of the outer circles, or, to use another expression, their reaching 'police maturity'. They had, presumably, reckoned with this process and even promoted it, knowing that complicity forges stronger bonds than any faith or ideal.

After the first month the prisoners became increasingly aware of this gradual change. The communiqué announcing the arrest of Rajk and his accomplices had already been issued, the population of the country had already demanded in panic-stricken spontaneity the liquidation of the imperialist agents, there were already signed admissions, compromising depositions. So the ÁVH leaders relaxed in self-confident calm while the initial wave of police-hysteria spent itself.

True, the statements and notes of the individual suspects seemed rather confused and did not fit together. But once these prefabricated elements were in the hands of the ÁVH *the first phase of the realization* could be regarded as complete, for the sole purpose of this first stage was to break down those under suspicion and extract from them statements involving themselves and their fellow-prisoners. It was the task of the *second phase* to weld together these elements and fill in any cracks that remained; the *third phase* had merely to add the finishing touches, the decoration and furnishing of the edifice and its solemn presentation to the public: that is, the preparation of the show-trial for public hearing.

Of course, not all those arrested passed simultaneously through the same phases of the *realization*. Often the phases overlapped. At times, during the first phase devoted to breaking down the prisoners, the ÁVH was able to accomplish the task of the second phase, too, and even the first contours of the building may have appeared for a moment behind the separate elements.

The physical and psychological instruments of compulsion applied during the first phase were not always identical. The intensity of the means depended not merely upon the measure of resistance shown by the prisoner, but also upon the degree to which the ÁVH regarded the prisoner's past and personality as important raw material. In such cases the physical brutalities were kept within certain limits in order to preserve temporarily, in usable condition, material considered valuable in the final construction of the trial.

When, after forty-eight hours of sleep I was taken back to the cellar, shaved and bathed, I had no idea that Gábor Péter had preserved me for an uncertain future, driven purely by the instincts of a thrifty craftsman, but even he could have had no definite notion how this raw material was going to be used. He could not have known, partly because, as it soon emerged, not the ÁVH but the MVD leaders decided how to mould the raw material, how to piece together all the elements. Gábor Péter could not have known, partly because he was in no position to include me in his calculations, as in my case even the first phase of the *realization* was not yet completed. I had made no compromising statement. I had denied being a spy, and even László Farkas's notes, dictated in my physical presence but spiritual absence, as I dozed on his floor that sunny June morning, were as yet unfinished.

The ambitious Colonel did his best to make up for lost time. As soon as I was back in the cellar he had me brought before him. This time his questions centred almost exclusively around László Rajk.

I spent many successive nights at the worn little table in his ante-room. The guard, leaning on his rifle, kept a careful eye on me while I described over and over again details of our university years, but more particularly of my later meetings with Rajk, a few private conversations we had after my return to Hungary, my official reports to him at the Ministry of Foreign Affairs. Whenever Farkas read my notes he raged aloud as though he were certain that while I was describing a few unimportant details, I was concealing the essentials. He was insistent that I should supplement my statement and make changes showing Rajk in a suspicious light. When, in the ensuing version, he again failed to find any damning allusions or phrases, he would make me re-write the whole story again.

I added nothing to the truth but neither did I conceal a single detail. Not, of course, in the hope of clarifying matters, for by now my former notion that if I stuck to the truth I might, to some extent, prevent the tangle of fact and fiction from growing, seemed puerile even to me; but I concealed nothing merely out of practical considerations, namely, to save myself and Rajk from a painful situation should our statements conflict. I felt that by concealing insignificant details we should lay ourselves open to the suspicion of hiding something important.

Therefore, I described how, in 1947, when I was editor of a weekly paper, and Rajk was Minister of the Interior, he tried to persuade me to leave my job and join the political police. As the idea did not in the least appeal to me, Rajk immediately dropped his proposal. Later, he proposed in the executive committee of the Communist Party that I should be appointed to the Ministry of Foreign Affairs. Not merely because he did not consider editing a weekly much of a job, not merely because I had attended the Academy of Diplomacy, but because he thought—and expounded this in detail—that there were too few Hungarian communists in the Ministry of Foreign Affairs who spoke foreign languages, knew the Western way of life and were able to maintain contact with Western people.

'Naturally,' the Colonel commented, 'it is characteristic of you that you wanted to maintain contact with the West.'

Then he interrogated me in great detail on the special tasks entrusted to me by Rajk when I travelled abroad. I had to account for my time practically from minute to minute, say what I had talked about with embassy employees, ambassadors, foreign diplomats, at receptions, dinners, or, as the Colonel put it, how I conspired. Farkas continually tried to make me admit that in 1948, when I went to Italy twice, once via Vienna, by train, once via Prague, by air, I did not stick to the prescribed schedule but made it my business to visit Yugoslavia.

In the second and third phase of the *realization,* such a statement, broadened and coloured, could have been used as proof that Rajk had indeed conspired with Tito, and had even used the opportunities presented by the Foreign Office for his purpose. But as yet, I had no idea that the aim of the trial would be to convict Rajk of such a conspiracy. I was merely filled with suspicion and surprise at the emphasis the Colonel put on this alleged trip to Yugoslavia, and the promises of the reliefs, benefits and food I would receive, should I admit it.

Then, a day or two later, I suddenly saw through Farkas's intention. I was just describing in my painstaking notes my only difference of opinion with Rajk. It took place at the Ministry of Foreign Affairs after the Cominform had expelled Yugoslavia from among its members and the Hungarian press had already launched its campaign against Tito. The ammunition for the attacks was supplied by the Hungarian Telegraph Agency, partly from its own information, partly from information received either from the party or from the Ministry of Foreign Affairs, which was pieced together by Foreign Office officials from the reports of the Hungarian Embassy in Belgrade; I had to decide whether, and in what form, to issue the information to the Hungarian Telegraph Agency. As the reports from the Embassy appeared wild, unreliable and often even fictitious I sometimes suppressed what was obviously false, not because I wanted to act against the party-line but because of my scruples as a journalist. Because of this the Minister reproached me on two occasions and, when I tried to argue, he declared that my attitude and resistance affected him like a cold shower.

On reading this part of my notes Farkas roared with laughter. This must be the exact opposite of what really happened, he said, only the opposite could be true, for Rajk had already admitted he was Tito's agent. I had better re-write my notes so as to show that Rajk had forbidden me to issue the anti-Tito reports. When, on the following day, I again declined to do this, Farkas triumphantly produced a typewritten statement from his desk. At the bottom of each page he showed me László Rajk's signature. Then he read me a paragraph of the statement. In this Rajk confessed to having been an agent of the Yugoslav secret service, and having furnished confidential information to Major Cicmil, head of the Yugoslav Military Mission, and to Ambassador Mrazov. Farkas turned the pages, then read me another paragraph in which Rajk admitted that in his student years he had joined the communist movement as a police *agent provocateur*. When my expression betrayed my disbelief, Farkas covered up the rest of the page and held both paragraphs before my eyes. Then he said:

'You see, there isn't much point in protecting your buddy. You can do him no harm now, whatever you say against him. You will only harm yourself if you continue to be so stubborn. I can assure you, His Excellency the Minister does not spare his friends.' Farkas turned more pages, then, as if he had found what he was looking for, he pronounced my name and added something in a murmur. 'Yes,' he looked up after a little while, 'Rajk has some very interesting things to say about you. Of course, I won't read them to you. We are waiting for your own confession. For that will show us your attitude to the Party, to the People's Democracy, and whether you are ready to help us. Then we shall deal with you accordingly.'

This was plain speaking with a vengeance. Farkas no longer demanded that I confess to the accusations which for weeks had served as a pretext for torture. For some time now he had mentioned neither Szönyi nor Wagner nor Field, and what was more, he had recently even dropped Colonel Karátson and the insinuation that I had been an agent of the pre-war political police. Now, Farkas no longer asked me for genuine or even invented facts, he asked me only for a *willingness to confess*, a readiness to put myself at the disposal of the ÁVH; that is, to make statements involving myself and others. He repeatedly stressed that it made no difference as far as Rajk was concerned what charges I brought against him. If the former Minister admitted that he had been a Horthy police agent and a spy, he would also admit what I accused him of. This assurance was intended to make me understand that there was no risk whatsoever, no matter how incredible the story I invented.

While I was busy writing my nightly notes, the Colonel ordered vegetables, and sometimes even meat for me, perhaps on the instructions of Gábor Péter or the doctor, perhaps in order to be able to blackmail me later by depriving me of food. During interrogations, he still placed his rubber truncheon on the desk, threatened me with it and sometimes hit me a blow, but in general he restricted himself to making me execute squatting exercises. It cost Farkas an obvious effort to restrain himself. At times, his eyes still assumed their glassy stare and his lips tightened in the rigid grin that, at the climax of a beating, used to distort this provincial garrison-officer's face so frighteningly, and although his hand reached often, almost unconsciously, for the 'people's educator', the beatings accompanied by bestial sexual utterances were not resumed. Farkas was now trying to come to terms with me, though not yet quite openly. He would not acknowledge that he was unable to produce any compromising fact against me and was, therefore, trying to establish a collaboration between our two imaginations.

'Look,' he would say, 'we know exactly what sort of fellow you are. We know exactly who your employers are, what espionage activity you were engaged in. It was the spy Rajk who tried to worm you into the people's democratic state security organization, it was the spy Rajk who insisted on your appointment at the Ministry of Foreign Affairs. Even the blind can see that you are Rajk's man, that you are birds of the same feather, that you can be nothing but a Horthy police agent and spy yourself.'

Here Farkas paused, then he added mockingly:

'Even if we didn't know all this, we could string you up whenever we wanted to on the basis of Szönyi's confession. We can wipe you off the face of the earth. As I said before, you shall dig your own grave and then a single bullet will fix you. But we never waste the public's money. We don't even need a bullet. In two years you will rot alive down there in the cellar. Shall I show you a fellow who has already been here for a year and a half?'

Without waiting for a reply, Farkas continued:

'All right. You shall see him. However, as we are not vindictive and are always rational in our thinking, we shall give you one more opportunity. You know what I mean, don't you?'

'I don't.'

'Of course you do. I've told you before. If you make a statement we shall sentence you to a short term in prison, then I'll send you to Spain to work for me there. But for that I need information with which to exert pressure. Information that will compromise you, so that I can keep you in check later. It is not enough that your family stays here. You must understand that.' He thought for a while, then, as if he had come to a sudden decision, he said: 'Now make a list of all your friends and acquaintances here and abroad who could have contact with British, Americans or Yugoslavs, and indicate which of them could be spies. We'll come back to Rajk later.'

'Some of my acquaintances did have contact with British, Americans and Yugoslavs but I have no knowledge of their having been spies.'

'Look,' Farkas replied with unusual mildness 'for the time being it is enough if you put down who, *in your opinion*, could have been a spy. Later . . . well, later we shall see.'

First I listed my friends living in Hungary. I scribbled for several nights but Farkas made a wry face every time he perused my notes.

'Isn't there a single spy among all these?' he asked gloomily.

'If there is, I'm not aware of the fact,' I replied cautiously.

'According to you, of course, everyone is honest?'

As I made no reply, the Colonel quoted a few names.

'These,' he said, 'have already confessed to having been spies. You must have known about them. And you did, too. But you deny it. You don't want to help us. I am warning you: you are heading for disaster.'

Then he made me list the names of my acquaintances abroad. The list was endless, as I had left Hungary as early as 1937, had spent two years in Paris attending the Sorbonne, writing articles, essays, short stories and, working as an assistant director in a film studio. In the course of these activities I had made many acquaintances and friends. And even more in South America. For, in 1939, a few months before the outbreak of the Second World War, I had signed an agreement with a French film company and had travelled to Argentina with a very advantageous contract in my pocket. But the war put paid to the French plans, so I wrote a screenplay for an Argentinian film company and then began taking photographs for advertising and catalogues. My active participation in politics began only when Count Michael Károlyi, whom I knew from my Paris days, launched a movement among Hungarians abroad to support the Allied war effort against Hitler, and for a new, democratic Hungary, to be created after the war. I joined Michael Károlyi's movement and soon became secretary general of the South-American branch.

After the collapse of the Habsburg monarchy, Michael Károlyi became President of the Hungarian Republic proclaimed in October, 1918, but when, in 1919, the communists seized power, Károlyi left Hungary. He lived in Vienna and Paris, and was at the outbreak of World War II, in London. In the eyes of the radical Hungarians living abroad, the integrity and political intransigence of the former President symbolized our democratic traditions, and also won him esteem and prestige in Western circles. The allies received our movement with approval and confidence, in South America, too. During the war years, in the course of various common enterprises, I came into contact, as secretary general of the Hungarian movement and editor of its journal, as well as in my private life, with British and Americans, Dutch, de Gaulle's French followers living in South America, Yugoslavs and anti-Hitler Austrians.

'Would you dare to allege,' Farkas asked, 'that there wasn't a single intelligence agent in these Inter-Allied Committees?'

'I wouldn't say that,' I replied, 'there may have been, but nobody dealt with me in that capacity.'

Farkas waved his hand dismissively.

'That's what you say, but I hope you don't imagine I believe it?' Then his face broke into a mocking smile, he breathed with relief and, like someone who had come almost to the end of a painstaking job but still had to apply the finishing touches, he asked me, 'And did you never talk with these Inter-Allied people about the affairs of the Hungarian movement?'

'Of course I did. We discussed and co-ordinated our common activities.'

'So, you informed them.'

'Yes, I informed them of everything that concerned them in the above mentioned connection. Delegated by the Hungarian movement's leadership . . .'

'That is, you informed them. You deliberately informed spies, therefore, *essentially*, you were a spy yourself.'

The same expression was used by the young ÁVH officer who devoted a whole night to a rhetorical explanation that the 'communists of Western orientation', though in the military sense not saboteurs or spies, were, with their Western mentality, bringing grist to the mill of the capitalist powers, and thus, *essentially*, were saboteurs and spies themselves. This *essentially* became one of the key-words of the ÁVH; it bridged the gap between the accusation and the supposedly capital crime. It served on innumerable occasions in the interrogation of innumerable fellow prisoners of mine to transmute harmless and insignificant deeds into crimes.

This formulation of a police conception had taken root in the jurisdiction of the Hungarian People's Democracy and the People's Court could sentence a prisoner at the bar on the basis of *presumption*. In various prisons, I came across many a prisoner sentenced to life imprisonment for trying to leave the country, but who instead of being charged with illegally crossing the border, was sentenced for espionage. Because, the indictment explained, had the accused succeeded in leaving the country it could be *presumed* that he would have contacted the espionage agencies of the Western powers and given them essential information concerning Hungary's internal situation and thus, *essentially*, would have engaged in espionage.

On the third floor of 60, Andrássy Street, I did not as yet anticipate this change in Hungarian legislation and therefore I entered into an argument with Farkas.

'It can under no circumstances be considered espionage,' I said, 'if someone discusses matters with his allies; besides, I never discussed with my foreign friends the disagreements within the Hungarian movement, or the regrettably frequent painful internal bickerings and intrigues among the emigrés . . .'

'Be kind enough to leave it to us to decide what is or isn't espionage,' Farkas interrupted, but with unusual politeness, feeling himself already in the saddle.

For the notes made during the last few nights and his endless interrogations had finally elicited certain details of my 'espionage activity'. As the Hungarian movement in Buenos Aires and our weekly paper possessed no addressograph, the office of the Inter-Allied Committee undertook, as a favour, to duplicate the list of subscribers to our weekly and at the same time also despatched to our subscribers the Committee's Spanish language publication. As most of the clerical and administrative work of the Committee was done by British citizens, I, according to Farkas, had, *essentially* handed over confidential papers of the Hungarian movement to the British espionage agency and as I had from time to time met the British head of the bureau and the British members of the Committee, Farkas established that I had maintained *contact* with the British *Intelligence Service*.

The term *contact* was the other magic word of the ÁVH. If an accused was even superficially acquainted with someone, he maintained *contact* with him. This is how I maintained *contact* not only with the spy and police agent Rajk but, by means of the addressograph, also with the British secret service; and one of my fellow-accused – a friend of mine since our teens – was compromised by the admission that he had *maintained contact* with me. With the help of this chain of *contacts* the ÁVH could link together dozens of accused – even if none of them confessed to a punishable offence – and could, *essentially*, make a mountain out of a mole-hill and turn a chat in a café into espionage activity. The sham-reality conjured up from a grain of truth by the magic power of the word *essential* was more ominous for the accused than the totally false charges. And because his fellow-accused, caught in a similar trap, gave up the struggle one after the other admitting, defeated, that *essentially* they were spies, the accused was compromised by having maintained *contact* with more and more spies until it appeared, in the end, as if he had exclusively frequented spies.

I know of numerous cases in which the accused, thus entrapped, was first subjected to the most violent methods of physical pressure, which then suddenly stopped and the lenient ÁVH officer appeared on the scene. From the very first moment of his first interrogation, this officer almost blushingly condemned the methods previously applied, adding, however, that the accused had to make allowances for the less sophisticated ÁVH men, since it was hard for anyone to believe that a man in the centre of an espionage ring formed by his friends and acquaintances, could preserve his integrity. This, at any rate, would be an alleviating circumstance. But the prisoner must think, he must try to remember. He would no doubt find evidence that others had taken advantage of his good faith.

While exploring such possibilities the mild ÁVH officer would offer the prisoner cigarettes, order him food, ask him if he was too cold in the cellar, whether he wanted a blanket. He would play the role of the warmhearted, humane man fulfilling a painful task, and sympathizing deeply with the prisoner. If it depended on him, he would release him. But the prisoner must see that there was certain circumstantial evidence against him. And if he did not comply, if he refused to help the ÁVH to uncover the details of the supposed conspiracy, those entrusted with the investigation might consider him obdurate, he might lay himself open to more suspicion and then even he, the lenient ÁVH officer, would not be able to prevent the application of violent measures.

The investigator and the prisoner would then consider, together, in what way the accused might have been used, naturally without his knowledge, how someone might have taken advantage of his good faith, and all the time the ÁVH officer would attempt to create a sort of benevolent complicity between himself and his victim. No sooner had they agreed on some kind of formula as a basis for an arbitrary interpretation, than the lenient ÁVH officer disappeared into thin air. The suspect was taken to another room, to another investigator, who looked him over grimly, appeared to know nothing of his ostensible good faith nor of the concessions made by his lenient predecessor. He turned the loose formula into a firm accusation, with the help of certain magic terms. He used the magic word *essentially*. If the prisoner had *maintained contact* with spies, he himself *essentially* became a spy. He then ordered the prisoner to account for his contacts.

Even if the accused was aware of the trap, he usually concluded from this changing of the guard that his situation was hopeless and he was now completely in the power of the ÁVH. It is quite possible that the chiefs of the political police applied this trick not because they hoped to deceive their prisoner but merely to make him realize how strong was the net in which he was caught, how hopeless any kind of attempt to free himself would be. All he could do was to resign himself to his fate, stop worrying about tomorrow and the day after tomorrow, because only the ÁVH could decide his fate, he himself could in no way influence the decision. He must accept the momentary advantages, the proffered benefits: the cigarettes, the food, the blanket, even the complicity with his interrogator. If he co-operated with the investigator in the drafting of a statement he might, perhaps, hope for clemency as a reward for his readiness to help. Why, for instance, should they deprive him of his life when they knew he was not really guilty and when, moreover, he had put himself at their disposal?

Many a prisoner arrived by way of considerations such as these, at the second phase of the *realization* and helped the ÁVH to piece together the prefabricated elements. As a result of his helpfulness he was, eventually, brought to trial charged with crimes so serious that his steps led from the court straight to the scaffold.

In my case László Farkas omitted to send the lenient ÁVH officer into the frontline. Not, I imagine, because he had no hope of achieving results by this method, but rather because the point of this exercise was merely to coax out the admission suitable for distortion of the truth. In my case, there was no need. Because, undeniably, in South America, I had been in contact with British people and this fact required only an insignificant addition, a slight turn, for *contact* to be reclassified as *espionage-contact*. However, to the Colonel's extreme annoyance, I was unable to bring myself to perform this short dance-step.

I regarded my position as hopeless and realized that Farkas might be right: that the court could pass sentence on me on the basis of Szönyi's statement, even though I denied it, and view the absence of a confession as an aggravating circumstance. Yet Farkas, who wanted to achieve quick results after having for so long made no headway, built too much on the magic word *contact* and made me recoil. For the Colonel insinuated not only that I had joined the British Intelligence Service in Buenos Aires and returned home upon their orders but also that in Budapest I was the *resident* of the British Intelligence Service.

This word I heard for the first time from Farkas's lips, having been rather unfamiliar with the terminology of the ÁVH and espionage affairs in general. But when I asked with interest, and not quite without malice, how I was to understand the word, Farkas told me to shut up and prescribed a good number of squatting exercises. From his following questions it became clear to me that the *resident* is a kind of chief spy who directs the activities of arriving, departing and local spies and collects and passes on information. If I admitted to having been a resident I should have to involve not only myself but obviously many others. Farkas must have been a poor psychologist if he believed that a man who had only survived thanks to the ill-mannered irony of fate, would be capable of shouldering the grave responsibility of exposing others to the sufferings he had experienced himself.

So I did not accept the complimentary appointment offered me, the position of resident, nor could I admit that I had carried on espionage activity in Hungary because that again would have started an avalanche of unpleasant questions. If I had carried on espionage activity, I relied, presumably, on informers and then the question would have arisen, who were they? Thus we got stuck with the *contact* I maintained with my British acquaintances and political friends and never reached the *essentially* formulation.

After many long nights of fruitless wrangling the Colonel resumed threatening me with the truncheon and pulled out once again the notes he had dictated on Péter Hain, Colonel Karátson and my activities as a police agent. It could not have escaped his notice that the accusation of having been a Horthy police agent filled me with greater loathing than the charge of espionage, and he may have hoped that should he insist on the former charge I would be more inclined to admit the espionage contacts. By now he was beginning his interrogations in the late afternoon, resting on his divan while I wrote answers to questions I had answered innumerable times before. My depositions began to assume the dimensions of a multi-volume novel.

As it happened, a very annoying and painful carbuncle had developed in my nose in those days, due to the lack of vitamins and cleanliness, for which, after waiting a full week, I had at last received some kind of ointment and a bandage. Wearing this almost mask-like bandage I was taken up, one afternoon, to Farkas's room. Followed by the guard I was trudging up the main staircase when at one of the turnings I came suddenly face to face with Gábor Péter. He was carrying a black attaché case; behind him were his body-guards. My guard grabbed me by the shoulder and turned my face to the wall.

'What has happened to you now?' I heard Gábor Péter's voice behind me.

I turned round and explained the bandage in a few brief words. Then it occurred to me that this was the least significant of the things that had happened to me, and, yielding to a sudden, obscure impulse, I added:

'I should like to ask you for a hearing.'

He looked at me, then motioned to my escort and his body-guards, upon which the ÁVH-men retreated a few steps, and kept a watchful eye on us beyond the range of our voices.

'Why?' Gábor Péter asked in a low voice.

I was at a loss for an answer; as a matter of fact, I didn't know why I had asked for a hearing, as it would be absolutely pointless to explain to Gábor Péter, of all people, that the charges brought against me had not a grain of truth in them. But now I was compelled to reply. I said, almost unthinkingly but with deliberation:

'Among other things because you know as well as I do that I have never been a Horthy police agent. Whatever happens to me I shall never, under any circumstances, confess to that charge.'

Gábor Péter looked at me again, more closely. Only much later did it occur to me that he may have taken my words as a promise to confess to the other charges. He nodded, deep in thought, then replied languidly:

'All right, you'll get your hearing.'

I entered Farkas's room after a longer than usual wait. The Colonel stood by the window opening on Andrássy Street, purple with fury.

'What did you want from the Lieutenant-General?' he bawled at me.

'I told him that I would on no condition confess to the charge of having been a police agent.'

'Do you think you're going to decide what you confess to and what not?' Farkas shouted and the veins stood out on his neck. 'Do you imagine you are at a country fair where you can choose among the boots on display?'

He stepped behind his desk and snatched his truncheon from the drawer, but he only gesticulated with it, then hit the top of the table several blows and commanded:

'Squat!'

He must have had a telephone call from Gábor Péter while I was waiting in his ante-room. Perhaps he had been instructed not to insist on the police agent charge but to try, rather, to concoct some useful material from my Western friendships and contacts. Whatever had happened, the statement prepared with much devotion and labour concerning Péter Hain and Colonel Karátsun was never mentioned again. Instead Farkas returned to my *contact* with the British.

He regarded it as proven that I had been an agent of the British secret service, and all he wanted to know now was who I had been in touch with in Hungary, what information I had received from them and by what means I passed on my information to my employers. When I denied having had any kind of espionage contact, Farkas, with admirable patience ignored my protest and put the next question, again in a way that assumed I had long ago admitted to having been a spy and was only withholding the details. He went on playing this psychological comedy for days and nights, at times orally, at times by dictating questions to which he demanded a written answer.

Farkas omitted the bastinado, spared my hands and kidneys and restricted himself to threats. He sucked lumps of sugar and only described to me with gusto, without ever applying them, the tortures conjured up for me in his imagination. Nevertheless, his interrogations were not less frightening to me than those that used to lead to the truncheon. Indeed, the Colonel's primitive play-acting struck me as more blood-curdling than physical pain. In the beginning, the period of guilelessness, I could still assume under the swish of the truncheons, that if I resisted they might recognize that they had been mistaken; later I could still hope they would realize that I was not the man to admit false charges or bring false charges against others. But now it seemed weightless in the balance of logic whether I admitted their accusations or not, for the ÁVH was deaf to any protest, argument or proof; for them, truth was a purely voluntaristic notion and in the end it would depend on the sovereign decision of the ÁVH whether or not an assumption, or a slander, no matter how stupid, would assume the status of incontrovertible evidence.

Therefore, although I had in fact admitted nothing, my situation was just as hopeless in this net of false facts as if the facts had been true, as if I had repentantly confessed that I had first been recruited by Péter Hain as a police agent and then had spied for Colonel Karátson, and had later become an agent of the British secret service in Argentina, had established contact between Tibor Szönyi and the American secret service, and finally conspired with the spy and *agent provocateur*, Lászlo Rajk, to overthrow the People's Democracy.

Never, in the interrogations, did Farkas omit to remind me of the trap in which I found myself and warn me of my helplessness. What was the point of resisting? After all, he insinuated, my chance of escaping, of remaining alive, depended on my showing some tractability, some pliancy. I must at least admit something, he would frequently repeat, sign something that could serve as a basis for the charges. Then they could transfer me to the prison controlled by the Public Prosecutor's department and sentence me. Otherwise, they would keep me here in the cellar for years. I should know better than anyone that I would not last long on the diet of the Andrássy Street cellar.

I did indeed know. I was spending my sixth week in the cellar on half a pint of soup and half a pint of beans a day. My strength was deserting me at a frightening speed, there was always blood in my urine, I could walk, or rather drag myself forward, only with the most painful effort and even at the most cautious movement my broken ribs hurt me. Therefore, compared with the ÁVH cellar, I imagined the prison of the Public Prosecutor's department as a kind of rest-home. A barred prison-window through which one could catch a glimpse of the blue sky or which permitted a sunbeam to penetrate, measured against my walled-up cellar-window, now seemed to me a Dolomites panorama, and the scanty daylight of a prison cell, compared with the lurid electric bulb in my cellar-hole, shone with the brilliance of the Italian Riviera.

I yearned for that prison the way an ordinary prisoner yearns for freedom. All this must probably have contributed to the shuddering loathing with which Farkas's face, voice and antics filled me. Not to have to see or hear the Colonel again was worth almost any price. Suddenly I caught myself wondering which of the suspicions voiced against me I should admit.

Farkas undoubtedly knew that, compared with my present quarters, prison must have seemed an idyllic place; he no longer promised to send me to Spain. Instead, he would say:

'Very soon we'll be sending a carload of prisoners over to the Markó street prison. If you make a statement, I shall include you in the group. If not . . . Well, you'll only have yourself to blame. I warned you, didn't I, that you were heading for disaster. Haven't I warned you a thousand times?'

He had indeed. What is more, his scareword, 'You are heading for disaster,' which he had always used unsparingly, had developed of late into a mania. He used it again to inform me that he had had enough of this dilatory sparring, would now send me down to the cellar and not have me brought up again for interrogation until I myself asked to be brought up to make a statement. It was absolutely indifferent to him whether it was months or years before I made up my mind. To me, however, it would not be a matter of indifference. And the Colonel really let himself go, describing in gruesome detail the symptoms of 'rotting alive'.

Like an artist gloating over his chef-d'oeuvre, Farkas tilted his head to one side, looked me over from top to toe, then remarked with mock pity that I must already have observed some of the symptoms of 'rotting alive' in myself; as he was more experienced in this field than I was he noticed it even more. Finally, he pointed his middle finger at the ceiling, stared at me grimly and shouted at the top of his voice:

'I am telling you for the last time: you are heading for disaster!'

After this, they really did not take me up for interrogation again. Farkas's theatricals had not helped my perplexity–which of the suspicions to admit–to ripen into decision. On the contrary, it gave me food for further thought.

At times it did seem rational that I should yield at least in part. But whenever I was able to divorce my thoughts from my miserable physical state, I knew that there was no escape from my irrational situation by the path of a logic that appeared–for the moment– rational.

I was not in a position to know the ultimate aims of the ÁVH, therefore I had to concentrate on a single rational effort: to preserve my physical and mental balance as far as I was able. If I obeyed Farkas's wishes I might, perhaps, gain physical advantages for a while. On the other hand, whichever of the accusations I admitted, I would have to name informers, collaborators, accomplices. If I were to follow in Szönyi's footsteps, I would, even if it meant more food and more sleep, lose my psychological balance because the realization that I had put a rope around the neck of others would quite surpass the limits of my moral endurance.

I think that my meditations were influenced in no small measure by the factor of my anger, and do not think I am mistaken when I ascribe this decisive word to it. I was nauseated by Farkas's repulsive play-acting and I felt it almost physically impossible to yield to such a man and thus, by yielding, justify his methods; yet I rebelled not only against Farkas, but much more against the institutions represented by him: the ÁVH and the Communist Party.

If the secret police allegedly discovered that many of my friends and acquaintances, concerning whose integrity I would always, even now, have put my hand in the fire, had been police agents and spies, it could only mean that they had undergone the same treatment as I had before they signed or failed to sign the false confessions. Thus, I could no longer regard my case as unique, the result of some sort of police-hysteria, but only as a part of a deliberate, even systematic, action initiated by the Party. When after soup-distribution, they led me to the lavatory I saw at least one dixie in front of each cell, an indication that the spy-factory was working at full capacity.

That long line of dixies was comical but at the same time revolting. The sight made me laugh, but it also made me clench my fists. Although there were still moments when I cherished hopes of a miracle thumbing its nose at reality, and proving that the last month and a half had only been a savage joke, a ruthless test, my temperament dismissed any temptation to ask for a meeting with Farkas.

Just when I was resigned to a long wait, suddenly, one morning, I was taken to the Colonel. Again his room was flooded with sunshine. But Farkas's face outshone even the sun.

'Well, how do you feel?' he asked me with a gay smile as if he had invited me in for a drink.

Not by a single word or a single hint did he revert to his earlier threats, nor did he repeat his statement that I could rot in the cellar for years, or that he would never have me brought up for interrogation until I myself asked to be fetched to make a statement. On the contrary, he was almost friendly. He asked me in a conversational tone about my acquaintances in South America, then made me write down again the names of those I had met and where, and what we had talked about.

He was particularly taken with the unusual name of a Danish teacher of backward children.

'This woman sounds suspicious to me' the Colonel declared and made me write a special report on her.

He requested more and more information and then I happened to mention the name of an Englishman who, if my recollections were correct, I had met at the teacher's flat. This Englishman took an interest in my private affairs with somewhat Castilian verve, at any rate with an enthusiasm unusual in the British, and tried to convince me with great eloquence and many arguments that I was committing suicide by returning to Hungary. Perhaps it wasn't even at Vera's flat that I met him; in any case, it was no more than a fleeting acquaintance. I had forgotten his name but often remembered his predictions during the last few weeks. It was not for the sake of a meticulous completeness of my report, that I mentioned him to Farkas, but because I was curious to see how my interrogator would react to the already more or less fulfilled prophecy. I figured that he would ignore it, or shout at me for provoking him with the stupidities of soothsayers and fortune-tellers. I was wrong. The opposite happened.

Farkas demanded an exact description of the Englishman, re-marking that to him it was as clear as daylight that my acquaintance had been an agent of the secret service, perhaps Vera's superior, because there was no doubt that the Danish woman was also working for the British secret service. These two had recruited me at Vera's flat. The Colonel demanded more and more details from which he could create an opportunity for the application of the magic word *essentially*.

He let me go in the middle of the night and this time he neither swore at me nor shouted impatiently that the interrogation had been fruitless.

'We shall continue tomorrow,' he said smiling at me gaily, amicably. 'Goodbye for the present.'

Next day I was not taken up for interrogation, nor did I see Farkas again. It was one of the basic principles of ÁVH methods that the prisoner must never know what is happening to him. He must constantly be given surprises, even sometimes relatively agreeable ones, as, for instance, the Colonel's façade of patient serenity when I expected the truncheon and more refined tortures or, at best, months of starvation in the cellar-hole.

It did not surprise me that I spent the twenty-four hours following the interrogation in my cell, but I was all the more amazed when on the morning of the second day they led me, through hitherto un-known passages, into a room I had never seen, photographed me from the front and the side, took my fingerprints, and then, with my face to the wall, made me stand in line in the corridor. I was just as astonished to discover in the line not only Otto Tökés, Rajk's former secretary, but also Péter Mód, counsellor in the Paris legation, Gyula Oszkó, former police Colonel, and even István Stolte who was living in West Germany and who could hardly have had any reason to return voluntarily to Budapest.

But I should have been even more staggered had I known then, that I had in vain refused to admit the accusations of having been a Horthy police agent and a spy, because from the higher point of view of the ÁVH I had completed the first phase of the *realization*:

though only rough-hewn, I was already a prefabricated element, a semi-finished product, a sort of building material, which would be used to glue together the polished, prefabricated elements in the *second phase of the realization.*

5

The Governor Appears on the Scene

OUR group was transferred to the Markó Street prison and–as far as I had the opportunity to observe–was put in cells on the same floor.

Compared to the cellar my new living-quarters were almost comfortable. There were two iron beds in it with straw mattresses, but neither a table, nor a bench, a chair or a shelf. Only in one corner did a lavatory pan proclaim the triumph of modern hygiene. However, I was disappointed in the barred window. Not merely because it was small and placed very high–I had expected that–but because its opaque frosted pane gazed down on me like a petrified, blind eye.

The dixie was handed in through an opening the size of a book cover and was approximately a foot and a half below the Judas-hole, which they kept locked. But when we were given fresh water the whole iron door swung open. It was unlocked twice, first when we put out the bucket, then when we took it in again. Only at such times did we see our guards face to face.

When the door of my cell flew open, unexpectedly, for the first time, four plain-clothes men stood in the corridor, shoulder to shoulder, glaring at me silently. Two were in their shirt-sleeves, a revolver-butt showing in their belts. For a while we looked at each other without a word. It flashed through my mind that one or another of Farkas's threats was going to come true when one of the gunmen spoke:

'Put out your bucket.'

As I moved to obey the instruction the three other men took a step backwards as if to cover their commander and one raised his hand to his belt. I don't know whether they were play-acting or whether this scene, too, proved that the heads of the ÁVH were trying to awaken a sense of danger in the outer circles of the secret police and make their uninitiated collaborators believe that they were facing implacable enemies.

Even if, under the influence of the adventure stories I had read in my childhood, it had occurred to me to attack the four guards, capture one of the guns and then break out through the multiple ring of armed men, my physical condition would have compelled me to postpone this romantic undertaking at least for the present. For I was still learning to walk. I rose from my bed moaning in agony, and at first considered it a remarkable achievement when I could stagger back and forth eighty or a hundred steps between the walls of my cell without stopping to rest. The food held out little promise that I would regain my strength. They gave us for the whole day half a loaf of sticky, black bread; in the morning a kind of dishwater made from roasted barley, at noon some thin soup and watery vegetable, and in the evening, a soup *called* vegetable. And of these only a tiny quantity.

Yet I could still have regarded the change as fortunate were there any sign to indicate that I was now a prisoner of the Public Prosecutor's department and that instead of Farkas and his colleagues, I would soon be brought before an examining magistrate sharing, perhaps, the convictions of the others but possessing more modest means of persuasion. Days went by and it was still armed plain-clothes security men and not uniformed prison guards who opened my door and handed in the food because, as I discovered later, the ÁVH had requisitioned two floors of the Markó Street prison for its own use and carefully isolated them from the rest of the prison. The prisoners of the Public Prosecutor's department looked with horror towards the ÁVH 'secret section', where no sound was ever heard except the clinking of the buckets and the slamming of feeding-holes.

The monotony of my days was soon interrupted by an agreeable surprise. The door was unexpectedly thrown open and the guards ushered in a burly man of medium size. The newcomer wore a conspicuously well-cut camel-hair overcoat and looked around shortsightedly before sitting down, opposite me, on the other bed. For a while he just sat there, gazing at his feet, then he rose, approached me and introduced himself:

'My name is Sándor Érdi,' he said, and began making sober enquiries concerning the prison and the prison rules.

He listened dejectedly to my report because, as he later admitted, he had hoped to find himself again in the custody of the Public Prosecutor's department as he had been on several occasions since 1945; he had presumed that I was some kind of gentleman burglar and not a political prisoner. Érdi went back to his bed deeply depressed, then he told me that until now, every time he was arrested by the Public Prosecutor's department, he had been able to obtain privileges by bribing the guards, had smuggled out letters to his lawyer and to his wife who had supplied him with food, cigarettes, clothes. But as a political prisoner, for now there was no doubt he belonged to that category, he could no longer hope to do much in the interests of his comfort, physical well-being and release. And yet . . . here Érdi began to tell me about the excellent relations he had had with some party heads, especially Károly Kiss, the secretary of the Communist Party's Central Control Committee. Suddenly he fell silent, paced the cell nervously, and finally stopped before me.

'Tell me, do you know who this Doolesh is?'

He pronounced the name with the long, Hungarian 'oo' and an 'sh' at the end, so that at first I didn't know who he was talking about. I shook my head and asked:

'Why?'

'Because they suspect me of having maintained contact with him.'

'What kind of contact?'

'What kind? Espionage contact, of course. When I was in Switzerland.'

'And who is this Doolesh?'

'Some American chief spy. How should I know who he is? I've never even heard the name before.'

Érdi raised both hands to his head with a theatrical movement, then collapsed on his bed and began to moan softly. I put various questions to him, to which he gave evasive answers. Later, he sat down beside me and told me in a whisper that they accused him of having been the contact man between the Deputy Minister of Defence, György Pálffy, and this Doolesh. Érdi had no doubt but that they had arrested Pálffy, as well, and that some unprecedented spy-trial was being prepared. In the course of our conversation it turned out that the man Doolesh, whose name Érdi had for the first time heard from his interrogators and – as they did – pronounced in a way distorted beyond recognition, could be none other than Allen Dulles, head of the American Intelligence Service in Switzerland.

My companion looked at me anxiously and asked in a shaky voice:

'What do you think? They wouldn't give me a death sentence, would they? After all, I am a nobody and even the accusation says I was only a contact . . .'

I tried to reassure him but Érdi interrupted our conversation time and again to request, now with tear-filled eyes, now with deep sighs, some words of comfort and an endless repetition of my assurance that they would not hang him. At times he wouldn't even wait for me to finish my little speech of consolation but would, without any preliminaries, launch into anecdotes, describe his home, his family, or certain scenes from his life, all with great emotion. I liked listening to him. Not only because, talking about the past, he forgot the miseries of the present and, temporarily at least, his continual lamentations, but also because Sándor Érdi's career, particularly in the period following 1945, threw light on facts and interdependences which I had never even suspected.

My cell-mate, like the other prisoners, had been deprived of his spectacles to prevent him from severing his veins with the broken lens or attempting suicide in some way. Imagining the gold-framed spectacles back on his face, and ignoring his crumpled suit, his tired, fear-worn features, I could see that had I come across him in a hotel lobby in the West and tried to guess his profession from his face and bearing, I should probably have hit the mark when I decided that this flabby, dumpy and yet dynamic, cheerful man could only be a not over-scrupulous businessman. And so it proved. Érdi was a racketeer in the classical sense of the word.

Not that he had started out that way. He was the child of poor parents and, as he himself related with melancholy irony, when young he thought he had struck it lucky when he got a job beating the keys of an adding-machine from morning till night. In those days he didn't wear a light camel-hair coat, but a black one and a black homburg and he regarded it as inconceivable that on a cloudy day anyone should leave the house without an umbrella. But fate had linked the little cashier with an equally insignificant actress who, to him, was the most beautiful, most wonderful fairy-queen in the world. For her sake he left his wife, his child and even his job. The little actress transformed him, or perhaps awakened his true nature. Sándor Érdi set out on the road of the businessman walking the sharp edge between the law and illegality. The Second World War had brought him financial success and by bribery and cunning he was even able to evade the consequences of the Jewish laws which spelled death for hundreds of thousands. But it was only after the war that his real career began.

In 1945 the devastated and despoiled country possessed neither food, industrial products nor transport vehicles. Thus it was that the government and the political parties not only tolerated semi-legal or even legally prohibited deals, but themselves formed enterprises whose business activities in any normal country and in normal times would have been stopped by the police and the Public Prosecutor. At last Sándor Érdi was in his element. He established an export-import firm. At a time when everyone who could smuggled in everything from locomotives to synthetic fertilizers, from cocoa to stockings, and trafficked in them, my cell-mate was well ahead in the race. Indeed, he became so eminent in the field that soon he was contacted by official personalities.

On one occasion, György Pálffy, who must have been keeping an eye on Érdi's activities, approached him with a strange proposition. At the time, Pálffy, a veteran and well-trained army officer who had played an active part in the anti-fascist resistance movement, headed the so-called military-political department of the army, that is, the defensive and offensive espionage services. He told Érdi that the state budget could not cover the expenses of the military-political department and therefore, naturally with the full approval of the Communist Party and his superiors, he was compelled to find the financial means himself. He proposed to Érdi that they should engage in some business deals in common. Érdi was to smell out possibilities and make suggestions as to how they could be carried out. Pálffy would help with the smuggling and back Érdi against the authorities should anything go wrong. After each deal they would share the profits. This proposal referred, of course, only to illegal deals, for the export firm could take care of the legal business, such as the sale of electro-meters to Damascus or the delivery of lavatory pans to Beyrouth without Pálffy's help.

Érdi accepted the profferred deal and for some time the partnership between the racketeer and the head of the counter-espionage service prospered admirably, to the satisfaction of both.

When Érdi recalled his most memorable exploits, his eyes lit up with pleasure; the day, for instance, when with the help of Pálffy's men, he had brought in, without paying duty, a freight-train full of goods, or the time when he sold wagon-loads of articles in scarce supply on the black market. But thoughts of the good old times cheered him only temporarily. Like the stage, when the footlights start to fade and dim, Érdi's face assumed a gloomier and gloomier expression until with drooping mouth he'd murmur plaintively:

'And now they are going to hang me . . .'

After my now almost ritual reassurance, my cell-mate would wonder in dreamy melancholy what his wife, the pretty blonde ex-actress, was doing at this very minute, where she was, what she was thinking about? Then suddenly he'd thrust out his chest, put his hands in his pockets, and, strutting up and down the cell, he'd explain with arrogant self-assurance, like a banker reviewing his investments, what in his individual transactions and deals should be regarded as original, even brilliant, what would never have occurred to anyone else – except Sándor Érdi.

'Of course,' he shrugged, 'I am an idiot. I should have stuck to the sort of thing I understood. Why did I have to stick my nose into politics?'

Érdi's involvement in politics took place one day when Pálffy made him sign a pledge recruiting him as an agent of the military-political department. What is more, and of this my cell-mate was rather proud, he was given army rank. Érdi, well-known as a racketeer in Budapest, was not a member of the Communist Party, nor did his undertakings reflect the triumph of socialist economy over private initiative, and for this reason he seemed particularly suited to win the confidence of bourgeois politicians. Therefore, Pálffy used his new man mostly for provocation.

My cell-mate told me how he had tried to ensnare the Small-holder Undersecretary of State, Pater Balogh, a reputedly corrupt man. He could remember the exact price of the cases of champagne and French cognac he had sent Pater Balogh, as well as the cost of the lunches and dinners consumed at 'Uncle Stern's' famous, though outwardly not very elegant-looking, Jewish restaurant. He told me how, instructed by Pálffy, he had tried to provoke General János Vörös, the former Minister of Defence, into compromising himself. By then, János Vörös had resigned his portfolio, after having been deserted in the Council of Ministers even by his Smallholder fellow-ministers when he protested against the draft of the Hungarian-Russian commercial agreement, on the grounds that, as he saw it, the agreement delivered the country economically into the hands of the Russians.

Well, Érdi approached the general and suggested that in the course of his frequent trips abroad he could take letters and messages for the general. Instructed by Pálffy, he brought up the name of a former Hungarian military attaché living in the West, who, or so the military-political department assumed, was working for the Americans. I can no longer recall whether Érdi did in fact smuggle letters back and forth between the general and the former military attaché or whether the attempt at provocation failed; but Érdi's description of the general's cautious mistrust stuck in my memory. Whatever happened, his caution did not save János Vörös from prison. Three years later we worked, facing each other, at the same table in the button-factory of the *Gyüjtö* and had alternate puffs at the same cigarette rolled in toilet paper.

Érdi's public activities were accompanied by decidedly more spectacular successess than this and similar attempts at provocation. His political moves were always directed by Pálffy. He was acting on the orders of the counter-espionage chief when he bought a lot of shares in the weekly *Kossuth Népe* and also, when after the disintegration of the Smallholder Party, he joined Zoltán Pfeiffer's Independence Party and in the 1947 elections ran for membership in Parliament on the Pfeiffer ticket. As he told me, he had put 40,000 forints into the election funds of the Independent Party, on condition that they nominate him as their candidate. This is how, at the last free elections in Hungary, an agent of the military-political department controlled by the Communist Party entered the Parliament building as a representative of the most unequivocally anti-communist political party. Later, on Pálffy's instructions, Érdi, whose erudition and political acumen were much below those of an average accountant, may have collaborated in the destruction of the Pfeiffer-party, and thus contributed to the final liquidation of the parliamentary system in Hungary.

Érdi's sometimes disconnected stories did more than give me a brief glance behind the scenes of public life. They brought to light other facts of which I had been just as unaware as I was of the smuggling backed by the authorities or of the agents planted by the authorities in the ranks of the opposition. What preoccupied me most – I had a notion it might influence our fate – was the conflict and competition which I now learned existed between the leaders and organization of the military-political department as well as the leaders and organization of the ÁVH and which was gradually turning into a life and death struggle. Although what my cell-mate had to relate did no more than awaken a well-founded suspicion, my conclusions were later confirmed by information gathered in prison.

Almost from the very first, the GRO (economic police department), which is similar to the Fraud Squad in Britain, working hand in hand with the ÁVO (State security department – predecessor of the ÁVH), attempted to thwart Érdi's and Pálffy's illegal deals. Érdi and his men were repeatedly arrested, and at such times, Érdi's wife turned to Pálffy and Károly Kiss to obtain her husband's release. Kiss was then head of the Communist Party's Central Control committee; it was his task to watch over the political and moral integrity of the Communist Party members. He knew about the agreement between Érdi and Pálffy; my cell-mate had repeatedly shown him copies of their accounts. Thus the high-ranking Party functionary could personally supervise both partners and ascertain that the racketeer was not cheating the counter-espionage chief, nor

99

the counter-espionage chief the Communist Party. It appears that Károly Kiss did not regard the heavy losses suffered by the state budget as an offence against communist morality for at the time the state was only partly in communist hands, and in order to seize it completely, it seemed expedient to strengthen the communist-controlled institutions. Therefore, Kiss interfered more than once to save Pálffy's agent from the legal consequences of the black-market deals, or even to stop an investigation into his affairs, and when he was imprisoned had him released–on orders from above.

After each arrest, the head of the GRO had Érdi brought before him and, before going into the merits of the case, offered to release him immediately, without further interrogation, if the racketeer pledged himself to work henceforth not for Pálffy but for him.

The military-political department and the economic police supported by the ÁVH would often arrest each other's men, try to annex each other's agents and extend their fields of authority. Originally the military-political department was entrusted with the work of offensive espionage and the ÁVH, as its most important task, with counter-espionage, that is, the removal of foreign spies. Undoubtedly, the two fields of activity met at numerous points, indeed, often overlapped and, under the conditions mentioned, clashes would have been unavoidable even under normal circumstances. All the more so as the ÁVH was linked to the Soviet MVD, and the military-political department to the counter-espionage and defensive service of the Soviet army, and there were, as it leaked out, conflicts and clashes of authority between the two Russian organizations, too. However, in 1948–9, motives beyond the obvious ones intervened in the struggle of the two Hungarian secret services and it was these motives that finally decided the battle.

The backbone of the military-political department was made up of anti-German officers of the old Hungarian army, men like Pálffy, well-trained officers versed in both the offensive and defensive services. Clearly, particularly in the early stages, the Russian military leaders had more confidence in these practised experts than in Gábor Péter, magically transformed from assistant tailor into police-general, for in the ÁVH, following the Russian example, every member was given military rank.

As in Hungary direct military considerations were gradually relegated to second place, and the maintenance of Moscow's chain of command became the most important consideration, the ÁVH was continually winning ground over the military-political department.

For it was the ÁVH, this organization formed in the meantime into a party within the party, that was called upon to execute the Russian seizure of power in Hungary. And as, from the point of view of the seizure of power, it was not professional knowledge that counted but reliability and loyalty to the Russian point of view, Gábor Péter easily triumphed over the old army officers, and the ÁVH over the military-political department. Whether or not the former officers would have been ready to subordinate themselves to the former tailor's assistant, they seemed, if not suspect, certainly capable of resistance, just like the old communists not disciplined by Moscow; they had therefore to disappear. This is why a few months after my meeting with Érdi, his employer, Lieutenant-General György Pálffy, joined Rajk in the dock.

Érdi was not in the least interested in these ramifications. The conclusions to be drawn from his stories and adventures left him cold, as cold as the fate of his likely victims. When I enquired how he would square things with himself if he learned that through him János Vörös had gone to the gallows, Érdi shrugged his shoulders:

'What else could I have done? Tell me what I could have done?' He spread out his arms and looked at me as an indignant adult might look at a child of hitherto irreproachable behaviour caught in an unforgivably stupid act.

Érdi considered himself a goodhearted, generous fellow and his eyes would fill with tears when he spoke of his family and the gifts he had showered upon them. He would have been not only astonished but indignant had anyone raised moral objections to his actions, for he was naïvely corrupt and harmed others by his fatuous harmlessness. It was with the same enthusiasm and unscrupulousness that he displayed in selling reject electro-meters to Damascus and damaged lavatory pans to Beyrouth, that he sold his fellow-men in Budapest. Thus, in his moments of panic, I could indeed have reassured him with even more sincere conviction; for after a bare two months course in the methods of the ÁVH, I could take it for granted that the People's Democracy would not hang Sándor Érdi, because it needed Sándor Érdi, the largest possible number of Sándor Érdis it could get.

Instinctively rather than deliberately I violated Hungarian prison etiquette where Érdi was concerned, because I did not call him by his first name, did not use this form of address to indicate recognition of our common fate. But even though we regarded each other as beings from different planets, even though it occurred to me that he had been put in my cell to spy on me, his stories not only enlightened me but also helped me to relax. I was fed up both with interrogation and with silence and he was the first person I had spoken to for a long time who had no authority over me and could not bully me. Thus, when one night our door was unlocked and I was ordered by our morose guards to put on my clothes and follow them, I felt not only apprehension at the thought of the unknown awaiting me, but also sadness at having to leave behind the familiar cell and even Érdi who had by now also become familiar to me.

While I was dressing my cell-mate watched me with pity and anguish, but as I walked out through the iron door he closed his eyes and kept them closed.

My guards took me down to the ground-floor and handed me over to two other plain-clothes security men. The latter handcuffed me, then made a sign to a uniformed gaoler, who came forward with servile haste to open the door. He raised his hand to his cap, but the ÁVH men paid hardly any attention to his salute. Even in the best of cases they treated the ordinary gaolers with arrogant condescension, as a feudal landlord might treat a flunkey.

A delightful breeze touched my face as we stepped out into the cool, starlit night. But I had no opportunity to look around as the ÁVH men pushed me hurriedly into the waiting car. My two escorts made me sit between them in the back and placed a pair of eye-shields lined with paper over my eyes. While the car sped across Margaret Bridge, and then took the steep mountain road, I could only think of Farkas's threats that, one night, they would make me dig my own grave and finish me off for having refused to aid the ÁVH.

Therefore I felt almost relieved when, just as on the first day of my arrest, I heard the wheels of the car rolling over gravel, when in the garage I smelled the odour of gasoline and finally when I set out with my two escorts down the stairs. In the cellar they removed the goggles, the handcuffs, searched me, then pushed me into the first cell. Hours went by but only the eyes of the guard appeared at regular intervals in the Judas-hole. It must have been late in the morning when they opened the door of my cell. Two guards led me to the familiar tower-room.

This time the windows of the hexagonal room were not covered in black curtains; they had only hung thick curtains over the lower three-quarters of them, but light and air penetrated into the room